Preserving Family Lands: BOOK I

ESSENTIAL TAX STRATEGIES FOR THE LANDOWNER

OCT 21

STEPHEN J. SMALL ATTORNEY AT LAW

Landowner Planning Center
Boston, Massachusetts

The purpose of this book is to alert landowners to the nature and extent of the potential tax and land-saving problems that may face them and their families, and to suggest possible solutions. No reader should undertake any of the suggestions described in this book without first consulting experienced professional advisors.

Tax and family land planning is an individual and personal matter for each landowner and for each family. Current financial circumstances and long-term financial goals differ, as do relationships between family members and different generations. Any single book cannot be, and this one is not intended to be, a substitute for individual tax and legal advice and planning.

Copyright© 1998 by Stephen J. Small, Esq.
All rights reserved.
Third Edition
First Edition published 1988
Second Edition published 1992

Cover design & art: © 1998 Gordon Morrison:
Licensed to Stephen J. Small, 1998
Interior design & typesetting: Marcia S. Miller
Desktop Design & Publication

Printed in the United States of America
Library of Congress Catalog Card Number: 98-066995
ISBN: 0-9624557-4-1
First Printing 10,000 copies

Landowner Planning Center
P.O. Box 4508
Boston, MA 02101-4508
Phone: 617-357-1644

Special bulk rates are available for the purchase of
Preserving Family Lands: Book I.
See the order form at the back of the book.

If you would like to be on the Landowner Planning Center mailing list for announcements about publications and other information, please write to us and let us know.

TABLE OF CONTENTS

INTRODUCTION TO THE THIRD EDITION

In 1988, I wrote *Preserving Family Lands* as a response to what I saw as a need for more simple, easy-to-read, *basic* literature about protecting the family's land. The book discussed some of the options that are available to land-owners, and the tax consequences associated with those options. I used a small number of examples to illustrate possible tax and land-planning problems and some of the possibilities that may be open to readers. What I tried to do was to cover *as simply as possible* a lot of the preliminary issues and questions that come up when a landowner begins to think about preserving his or her land.

I had no idea what a need there was!! Some readers have told me that this is the most important book in its field in at least the past decade. The first edition, published in May of 1988, sold more than 50,000 copies, in all fifty states and even abroad!! The second edition, published in 1992, sold another 30,000 copies. This book enabled land-owners to preserve thousands and thousands of acres of important land all across the country.

The time has come to revise and update the original *Preserving Family Lands*. Much of the text remains the same, although this third edition includes current income tax rates and estate tax rates, as well as other minor revisions. This edition also includes a discussion of an important new estate tax incentive that passed Congress in 1997 for landowners who donate conservation easements. I have also included a number of design changes and I hope you like those.

As with the prior editions, there are a number of things this book *will not* do. It will not go into all of the intricacies of the income tax or the estate tax. It will not go into all types of charitable giving. It will not cover all of the state and federal incentives and programs that are available to landowners, either in the tax law or through other means, to help preserve the family farm or ranch. It will not tell you how to convince reluctant family members to protect the family's land and save taxes, although it will give you information and ideas that may help you if such convincing becomes necessary. This book will not discuss all of the planning options and will not answer all of your questions.

However, there are quite a few things this book *will* do. It will give you information about land-saving choices. It will give you information about how you can combine saving land with saving taxes. It will help you find the right advisors if you decide to go ahead with preserving your family's land, and it will help you ask those advisors the right questions.

Many people who have read *Preserving Family Lands* told me they would also be interested in a second book, dealing with more advanced planning concepts that were not covered in *Preserving Family Lands*. In 1997, I wrote *Preserving Family Lands: Book II – More Planning Strategies for the Future*, to meet this need. *Preserving Family Lands: Book II* is not an "update" or "revision" of the first book. It is really the second book in the series. *Preserving Family Lands: Book II* really focuses on what I call "succession planning for the landowner." Succession planning includes not just easements but also the estate and gift tax rules, basic rules about partnerships and trusts, how the planning process can work for complex family lands situations, and more. See Chapter 9 of this book for more on "Book II." We've sold more than 10,000 copies of "Book II" since its publication last year.

In addition, in an effort to help make the point that *Preserving Family Lands* (this book) and *Preserving Family Lands: Book II* cover different material, I have made a slight name change to this book and it is now titled *Preserving Family Lands: Book I*. *Preserving Family Lands: Book I* is the same as the original *Preserving Family Lands*, revised and brought up to date in this 1998 third edition.

I would like to thank all of the people and all of the groups around the country who purchased the first two editions of *Preserving Family Lands*. I would like to thank all of the readers who have written to me with letters of thanks for helping them to preserve their own important land and for enabling them to pass the word on to others about how to help preserve the quality of life in their communities. Thanks to my daughters Stephanie and Victoria for their encouragement and support. Finally, thanks to my wife Connie for her invaluable and continuing editorial, logistical, and general-contractor assistance to help put this book together.

S. J. S.

What Happens If...

The chart below summarizes in very brief form what happens to John and Mary and their property, Riverview, under different possibilities discussed in this book.

What Happens If John and Mary:	Income Tax Savings?	Estate Tax Savings?	What Happens to Riverview?
Leave Riverview to the children in their wills (Chapter 1)	No	No! Catastrophe!!	Forced sale for development
Make a gift to charity now of an easement on Riverview, and then leave Riverview to the children (Chapter 3)	Yes	Yes	Riverview goes to the children and will be protected
Make a gift to charity now of a remainder interest in Riverview (Chapter 4)	Yes	Yes	Riverview goes to charity and will be protected
Make a gift to charity of Riverview, or of an easement on Riverview, in their wills (Chapter 5)	No	Yes	Riverview will be protected
Give Riverview to the children now (Chapter 6)	No	Yes	Riverview might be protected
Sell Riverview now, for cash (Chapter 7)	No!!	No!!!	Sold for Development

CHAPTER 1

The Estate Tax: An Eye-Opener

John and Mary and Riverview

John and Mary Landowner are very lucky people. Twenty-five years ago they bought Riverview, a 200-acre estate, for $100,000. The value of Riverview crept up steadily for a decade after that and has skyrocketed in the past fifteen years.

John and Mary are in their sixties now, and they love the quiet at Riverview, the gently rolling hills and open fields. Although Riverview lies in the path of increasing suburban sprawl, the Landowners would like to see their property permanently protected. A developer recently offered them $2,500,000 for Riverview, but they turned him down. The land is too important to them to sell out, and they are planning to leave Riverview to their children, along with the $1,500,000 in other assets John and Mary have accumulated.

The Landowners both have wills, drawn up some years ago. Under their wills, the first to die leaves everything to the survivor, and, on the death of the second spouse, the children inherit the estate. Let's see what happens.

Let's assume that John dies first. Under the federal estate tax laws, there is little or no federal estate tax due at that time. When Mary dies, these are the results, keeping in mind that she has Riverview, worth $2,500,000 (likely to be worth more than that because of future appreciation), and $1,500,000 in other assets.

- The federal estate tax on her $4,500,000 estate is $1,358,350. In addition, if the Landowners lived in Massachusetts, or California, or South Carolina, the estate tax due to the state would be $280,400. Total tax due? $1,638,750!

- *Riverview must be sold to pay the estate tax.* The estate tax is due nine months after Mary's death, so the family may not even be able to wait for the "best" offer.

- Once Riverview is sold for development, the gently rolling hills and open fields will be gone forever. *The future of Riverview is completely out of the hands of the family.*

Bob and Sue and Diamond Farm

Bob and Sue Farmowner own Diamond Farm, 500 acres that Bob's father bought in the 1940s for $50 an acre. It has been farmed by the family since that time. All of the family's energy, and almost all of the family's cash, has been poured into the farm. In addition to Diamond Farm, they have about $200,000 in cash and stocks, most of that inherited from Sue's parents.

Bob and Sue are in their late fifties now. They have been offered $1,700,000 for Diamond Farm by a local real estate developer, and they know there are other things they could do that might make life a little easier for them. However, they are proud of their way of life and  what they have been able to build up. It gives them a lot of pride, too, to know that their children want the farm to stay in the family so they can follow in Bob and Sue's foot-steps. Bob and Sue certainly don't feel like millionaires, but their prime agricultural land on the urban fringe puts them into that category.

Under their wills, drawn up some years ago, the first to die leaves everything to the survivor, and, on the death of the second spouse, the children inherit Diamond Farm. Let's see what happens. (There is a special federal estate tax valuation program for farms, and Diamond Farm and the Farmowners' estate might be eligible. The purpose of this example, however, is to point out the awful result that occurs if that program is not available or not used, or if a family is unwilling or unable to continue to farm the whole property.)

Let's assume that Sue dies first. Under the federal

estate tax laws, there is little or no federal estate tax due at that time. When Bob dies, he thinks he leaves Diamond Farm and the $200,000 in other assets to the children. This is what happens:

- The federal estate tax on his $1,900,000 estate is $441,350. In addition, if the Farmowners lived in Colorado, or Virginia, or Florida, for example, the estate tax due to the state would be $92,400. Total tax due? $533,750!

- *Diamond Farm must be sold to pay the estate tax.* The estate tax is due nine months after Bob's death, so the family may be forced to take less than they expect.

- Once Diamond Farm is sold for development, one more fertile, working farm will be gone forever, along with its contribution to the nation's food and fiber and its contribution to the region's open space. *The future of Diamond Farm is completely out of the hands of the family.*

You May Have a Problem, But You Also Have Choices

Most people certainly aren't as comfortable as John and Mary and certainly don't have land as valuable as Riverview. Most people don't have land as valuable as Diamond Farm, either. *But I use these examples to illustrate the devastating effect the estate tax system can have on a family's land and a family's plans.*

This book will make two important points. The first point is that many of you, like the families I have mentioned, are facing a potentially significant *estate tax* problem, because in many cases, a major portion of your estate is a *very valuable* piece of land. Even if you have property that is significantly less valuable than Riverview or Diamond Farm, you still may be facing the same problem. FOR THE FIRST TIME IN THE HISTORY OF THE UNITED STATES, THE FAMILY THAT JUST WANTS TO LEAVE ITS LAND TO THE CHILDREN MAY NOT BE ABLE TO DO THAT. The land may have become so valuable it may have to be sold to pay the estate tax.

The second point is that there is, in fact, something you can do about this problem. You do have choices.

Preserving Family Lands

CHAPTER 2

Where Do We Begin?

The Problem

We can begin with an understanding of the problem.

Simply put, the problem is this: without proper planning, a valuable piece of land in an estate can trigger an estate tax so large that the land itself will have to be sold to pay the estate tax. If it is important for the family to preserve the land and to have a manageable estate tax bill, the lack of proper planning can lead to a terrible and irreversible result.

For the community that cares about protecting the quality of life, the federal estate tax may be the biggest single threat to the protection of farmland and forestland, watershed, open space, wildlife habitat, and scenic vistas. FOR THE FAMILY THAT CARES ABOUT ITS LAND, THE FEDERAL ESTATE TAX MAY BE THE BIGGEST SINGLE THREAT TO THE FAMILY'S LONG-RANGE PLANNING.

Why does this potential problem exist for so many families today? I think there are four reasons.

First, the dramatic increase in land values, particularly over the past decades, has added wealth, in some cases enormous wealth, to many families. Bob and Sue Farmowner are only one example of thousands of families that are now land rich and cash poor, heading for a major estate tax shock and setback.

Second, federal *estate tax rates* remain high, and are now especially high when compared to federal income tax rates. The highest effective federal estate tax rate is *above 50%*; the highest federal income tax rate is now almost 40%. All of the increase in value of Riverview continues to be taxed at a *very high* estate tax rate.

Third, part of the problem is that an increasing number of families want to protect the family's land. The family land conservation ethic wasn't quite so strong when it was easier to find a pretty, tranquil place to live, or a desirable ranch or farm, when so many nice pieces of property had not yet fallen victim to the bulldozer and the subdivision. How many times have John and Mary Landowner said or thought, "Why, we couldn't find another place like this one, and if we could, we couldn't afford to buy it."

The fourth part of the problem is that, unfortunately, too many families and too many family advisors *do not recognize* that a valuable piece of land in a family's estate requires special attention and a special kind of estate planning. This could be so for a variety of reasons. Possibly it is not apparent how valuable the land has become. Possibly the land is simply treated as "value" in the estate; if there is an equal amount of "value" of *stock* in an estate, it may hurt to pay the tax but it is unlikely that selling the stock will lead to teardrops on the family's scrapbook. *The standard, even sophisticated estate plan, certainly in Bob and Sue Farmowner's case, often will not protect the family's land.*

What can Bob and Sue Farmowner do? What can John and Mary Landowner do? What can you do?

Planning for That High Value

As you read through this book, think about the high value in your land. John and Mary don't want to sell Riverview to a developer, but Riverview's development potential, that "extra" value, can create significant problems for their estate. Instead, if they plan properly and are smart, they can give away that value, lower their estate taxes, and potentially generate an income tax deduction. The income tax deduction almost seems like a bonus.

The same is true in Bob and Sue's case. Diamond Farm is not worth more than a million dollars as a farm, it is worth more than a million dollars as the beginning of a subdivision. If Bob and Sue can afford to and are willing to forego the *very real dollars* that could come to them from a cash sale, they can turn that high value into a tax benefit, *and* preserve the farm for their children.

Important Questions for You

■ Is this high value a problem for you? Can it be used to your advantage?

■ What are your assets and debts?

■ How high is the value of your land compared to the rest of your net worth?

■ Is your land likely to increase in value significantly?

■ Does your land have development potential?

■ Do you have an estate plan? Does the estate plan give special consideration to your real estate?

■ Do you know how high the estate tax will be on your estate? See the Landowner's Quiz at *Appendix A* and the Estate Tax Tables at *Appendix B* for some help with that question.

What do you want to do?

■ Do you want to cash in on the value of the land?

■ Do you want to see your land subdivided or turned into a shopping mall?

■ Do your children want to see the family land protected?

■ Do *you* want to see the family land protected?

■ Do you want to keep your land or give it to charity?

The next few chapters will present some of the possibilities for you. The federal tax laws provide a variety of incentives for land conservation. Those incentives run from keeping your property but imposing restrictions on its future use, to giving away your property to charity at some point in the future, to giving your property to charity immediately.

If you plan right, and take advantage of these incentives, you can accomplish three things. First, you will have protected your land from the developer's bulldozer. Second, you can lower the value of your land for estate tax purposes (or the value of your estate if you give away all or a portion of your land). Third, when you give away that value, you are entitled  to an income tax deduction that potentially can bring you substantial tax benefits now. With proper planning, by lowering the value of your land and lowering your estate tax burden, it may be possible for your family to avoid selling the land at all.

Some of the Choices--
Do you want to keep your land, and protect it?

You may be entitled to an income tax deduction for *protecting your property from development*. That protection takes the form of a recorded restriction on your property, known as a "conservation easement" or a "conservation restriction." When you create and donate a conservation easement to a charitable organization *you still own your land*; the size of the income tax deduction is based on the *value of the development rights you give up*. In addition, since you are reducing the value of your property, the value of your taxable estate drops, your estate tax drops, and your property tax should be lowered. I discuss conservation easements in Chapter 3.

With a conservation easement, you have restricted your right (and the right of any future owner) to develop the land, but you can continue to live on it or farm it, invite guests over or keep trespassers off, or, subject to the restrictions, sell the property, give the property away, or leave the property to your children.

Do you want your land, or a conservation easement, to go to charity, but not until you die?

A second tax incentive for land conservation is a "remainder interest." With a remainder interest, a land-owner retains the right to live on his or her land until death, and at death the land goes to the charitable organization. Chapter 4 is on remainder interests.

The gift of a conservation easement or an outright gift of property may be made during the donor's lifetime, and may qualify for an income tax deduction, or the gift may be made in the donor's will. A gift by will is called a "testamentary" gift. If the gift is made in the donor's will, there will be no income tax savings, but the value of the gift will not be included in the donor's estate for estate tax purposes. Gifts by will are discussed in Chapter 5.

Do you want to keep your land in the family but get it out of your estate?

A further possible approach to family land planning and estate planning involves giving your property to other family members while you are alive. A lot of incorrect thinking exists about this subject. In Chapter 6, I briefly review gifts made to family members while you are alive.

Do you want to sell your land now, and cash in on that high value?

Chapter 7 is devoted to a comparison of the rather surprising dollar results if John and Mary sell Riverview to a developer for its maximum development potential or if they put a conservation easement on Riverview but reserve the right to create four more house lots.

What else do you need to know?

Chapter 8 covers, briefly, some of the other things a landowner will have to do and keep in mind to get from here to there.

In Chapter 9 we step back a little bit and take a look at the major problems facing family landowners today and what I see as the solution to those problems. In addition, in Chapter 9 there is a very brief discussion of other related planning tools that are discussed in another book you may be interested in, *Preserving Family Lands: Book II – More Planning Strategies for the Future.* I wrote "Book II" in 1997; you may want to read that once you have finished this book. There is an order form for both books at the end of this book.

Chapter 10, I hope, will help you get started.

As I mentioned earlier, Appendix B to this book includes Estate Tax Tables that will give you an idea of what the total federal and state estate tax will be on your estate.

Appendix C covers a special tax rule that may be helpful to some people who make charitable contributions.

Appendix D explains a very important estate tax incentive for voluntary, private land conservation.

You can't just do nothing

A generation ago, or even a decade ago, a landowner who cared about his or her land didn't have to do much tax or legal planning, and in many cases didn't have to do *any* tax or legal planning, to see to it that important family land made it intact to the next generation of owners.

A lot of you who are reading this book *don't like to be told what to do with your real estate.* But listen carefully: if you *don't* take some action, if you *don't* begin planning now, *the government is going to tell your family what to do with your real estate and your heirs aren't going to like what they hear.*

The planning will be different for every landowner and for every family. The planning may go well beyond some of the choices and suggestions in this book. But if you care about your land, and if your land is valuable, and if you want to keep your land intact and pass it to the next generation, *you can't just do nothing.*

Once again, some of the choices

Once again, some of the choices: a conservation easement, a remainder interest, a gift by will, gifts to other family members while you are alive, a cash sale. Which one is right for John and Mary? Or for Bob and Sue? Or for you?

Let's look first at conservation easements.

Preserving Family Lands

CHAPTER 3

Gift of a Conservation Easement

What is a "Conservation Easement"?

Put very simply, a *conservation easement* is a restriction on the use of your property. It is a *recorded deed restriction*, and the *right to enforce the restriction* is given to a tax-exempt charitable organization (generally in the conservation field) or a government agency.

In its most basic form, a conservation easement *will protect* land against future real estate development, industrial use, and many potential commercial uses. A conservation easement generally allows you to *continue current uses*, including, for example, residential and recreational use, agriculture, forestry, or ranching. A conservation easement protects *some important conservation quality* of your land, such as habitat, open space, or scenic views.

Sometimes a "conservation easement" is also referred to as an "easement" or as a "conservation restriction." In this book I use the terms interchangeably.

There is more on all of this throughout this book, but this is enough to get you started.

Background

You have the right to do a lot of different things with your property. Subject, of course, to local zoning and public health and safety requirements, a property owner can plant trees or cut them down, build buildings or demolish them, grow crops or raise cattle, grow peonies, dig holes in the property, fence the property in, build a wall around it, and so forth.

The gift of a conservation easement to a charitable organization involves voluntarily giving up *some* of these rights (such as the right to build condos all over the land) and putting in the hands of the donee organization the power to enforce the restrictions on the use of the property. Remember, if you donate an easement you are only limiting *some* of your rights with respect to your property. As I mentioned in Chapter 2, *you continue to own your land*, and you can do anything with your land that is not prevented or restricted by the easement.

Every landowner is unique and every piece of land is unique. Every conservation easement should be unique and must be tailored to meet the needs of *that particular landowner* and *that particular piece of land*.

The "Conservation Purposes" Test

It is important to emphasize that not every easement restricting the future development of property will meet the tax law requirements. The tax law requires that the gift be "for conservation purposes." As a rule, the following generalization works: the more significant the land is, the more it adds to the public good, the more likely it is that you will qualify for the deduction. If you are protecting a large tract of primarily undeveloped property (like John and Mary Landowner) or ranchland or farmland (like Bob and Sue Farmowner), or a smaller parcel of land with scenic or open space qualities, if you are protecting habitat for an important or threatened animal or plant species, if you are preserving a scenic view on a long stretch of roadside that is threatened with subdivision, if you are contributing to a greenbelt around a city or preserving a watershed by a scenic brook or river or lake, your donation is more likely to qualify for a deduction. In addition, you can meet the "conservation purposes" test if you protect important historic property.

You will probably *not* qualify for a deduction if there is nothing special or unusual about the land that you are protecting except that it does not currently have more houses on it. Think of it this way. *If you are truly contributing something to the general environmental well-being of the area, then that's a good (and deductible) gift.* If you are truly trying to get away with something ("maybe I can get a deduction for not permitting any more development on my suburban house lot"), and there is nothing particularly unusual about your property or its setting, you are probably not entitled to an income tax deduction. (As a practical matter, in this latter case, it may be difficult to find a donee organization to accept your easement gift. See Chapter 8.)

If you are in doubt about whether or not an easement on your property would qualify for an income tax deduction, see Chapter 8 *for some of the people who can help you answer this question.* In many communities around the country, local tax-exempt organizations have been formed precisely for the purpose of protecting open space and other important land in the area. These organizations, often called "land trusts," should be in a good position to assist you.

One final important point about a conservation easement. In many cases it will be possible to qualify for an income tax deduction by giving up the right to develop your property to the maximum possible extent *while still retaining the right to do some limited development in the future.* If a conservation easement preventing any further development on John and Mary Landowner's Riverview would qualify for an income tax deduction, John and Mary could also reserve the right to build, for example, four more houses on Riverview, subject to certain restrictions and limitations, and still qualify for an income tax deduction as long as the property's conservation values continued to be preserved. Remember, however, that in many cases conservation values and *any* further development will be incompatible.

How the Gift is Valued

For purposes of the tax rules, the "value" of a property is equal to what it would sell for if it were put to the most valuable economic use that is possible under the circumstances. In many cases (though not all), with land that is generally undeveloped or only partially developed, the "value" for estate tax purposes is equal to the highest amount someone would pay for it if it were sold for development.

Let's say that Riverview is worth $2,500,000 to a developer (who would then subdivide the property, build homes on it, and sell homes and/or house lots).

If Riverview were subject to a conservation easement, however, and *could not be subdivided*, the development potential would be non-existent and the value of the property would be considerably lower (although Riverview would still retain some significant value). For example (and remember, this is just an example), let's say the value of Riverview as a 200-acre "estate" that could never be further developed is $1,000,000. For the Landowners' property, then, the value before the easement or restriction would be $2,500,000, and the value after the restriction would be $1,000,000.

Now, here is the rule. In the case of a gift of a conservation easement, *the value of the gift is generally equal to the difference between the value of the property before the easement and the value of the property after the easement.*

Using the example above, the value of Riverview before the easement or restriction is $2,500,000, the value after the restriction is $1,000,000, and that means *the value of the gift is $1,500,000. That represents the income tax deduction John and Mary are allowed,* subject to limits discussed below.

Consider another possibility for John and Mary. As I suggested earlier, as long as Riverview's conservation values continue to be protected, John and Mary could donate a conservation easement on Riverview and *still retain the right to do some limited development on Riverview in the future.* For example, they could donate a conservation easement on Riverview and reserve the right to build four more houses there, subject to certain restrictions and limitations. In this limited development possibility their house and lot could be worth $900,000 and each of the four "reserved" lots could be worth $150,000. The total value after the restriction would be $1,500,000 ($900,000 plus the four lots at $150,000 each).

In this example, the value of Riverview before the easement is $2,500,000, and the value of Riverview after this easement is $1,500,000, so the value of the gift is $1,000,000 ($2,500,000 minus $1,500,000).

For Bob and Sue Farmowner, a conservation restriction on Diamond Farm would likely have a similar, dramatic effect. If Bob and Sue donate an easement that restricts the future use of Diamond Farm to agricultural and/or ranching uses, they will significantly reduce the value of Diamond Farm.

Diamond Farm will now be valued as *farmland* (say that's $1,000 an acre in their area) rather than as a potential subdivision. With Diamond Farm worth $1,700,000 *before* the easement, and $500,000 ($1,000 an acre) *after* the easement, the value of the easement is $1,200,000. Their income tax deduction, then, is $1,200,000.

The ability of any family to use these deductions for income tax purposes is limited, as discussed below. But John and Mary have "given away" much or all of that *development value* that was pushing their estate tax so high, the Farmowners have reduced the value of their estate by more than $1,000,000, and both families can continue to own, use, and enjoy their family land. If either family at any point does decide to sell, any future owner will be subject to the same restrictions, *and Riverview and Diamond Farm can be saved.*

The Income Tax Deduction

No matter how much any individual gives to charity, limitations in the tax law make it impossible to eliminate the total amount of federal income tax due.

Let's start with an example.

If John and Mary have annual income of $200,000, even if they make a gift to charity this year of an easement valued at $1,000,000, their tax deduction for the year of the gift *is limited by the tax rules* to $60,000 (30% of their $200,000 income). The "unused" portion of their gift ($940,000) remains available to be "carried forward" and used as a deduction against their income for each of the next five years.

Here is the general rule. A donor can only deduct the value of a gift of land, or of a conservation easement, or of a remainder interest in land (see Chapter 4), *up to* 30% of the donor's income for the year of the gift. Any amount of the gift remaining after the first year can be carried forward and deducted against income for the following five years.

There is one significant exception to this rule. In certain circumstances it may be advisable to take advantage of a special rule in the tax law that potentially can help you generate *higher* income tax benefits than those I have discussed above. All the details of the *gift* would be the same, only the tax calculations would change. See Appendix C for a discussion of this special rule.

Finally, note that when the dollar value of the easement gift is significantly higher than the donor's annual income, the 30% limitation may make it impossible to "use up" all of the deduction. In the above illustration, using John and Mary's easement donation valued at $1,000,000, if John and Mary's income remains the same each year, only $360,000 of the gift ($60,000 in the first year and $60,000 for each of the five carryforward years) will be "used up." The bad news is that the full $1,000,000 value of the gift cannot be  used to generate *income tax savings*, because only $360,000 can be deducted under the 30% limitation rule. The good news is that the entire reduction in the value of Riverview is, for John and Mary, an essential first step toward *protecting* Riverview, *avoiding* an enormous estate tax bill, and *leaving Riverview to their children.* (For more on the additional planning steps John and Mary might take, see Chapter 9.)

Example: John and Mary

John and Mary have a current combined annual income of $200,000 and $40,000 in itemized deductions.

They estimate that, not including Riverview, their estate is valued at $1,500,000.

They purchased Riverview, their 200-acre estate, when the area was mostly rural; they paid $100,000. "Suburban sprawl" has made Riverview one of the few remaining local tracts of open space, and that has also made it attractive to developers. Riverview could easily be subdivided and sold off, and the property is now worth $2,500,000.

Working with their advisors (advisors who understand the problems and opportunities and who understand what John and Mary are trying to accomplish; see Chapter 8), John and Mary donate a conservation easement on Riverview to a charitable land conservation organization. In the easement, they reserve the right to keep their house and a large lot and to create (and sell) four additional house lots on Riverview, located in such a manner to protect, to the maximum possible extent, Riverview's important conservation qualities.

Assume that the main house and lot is worth $900,000 and that each of the "reserved" lots is worth $150,000, for a total remaining value of $1,500,000 for Riverview after the easement gift. That gives John and Mary a $1,000,000 charitable contribution.

To make the calculations easy, assume the Landowners' income and deductions are the same for the next five years and that their deductions include $10,000 for state income taxes, $10,000 for property tax, and $20,000 in mortgage interest.

Note in the "Without the Donation" table below, instead of a total of $40,000 in deductions, John and Mary are only allowed $37,636. This is generally because of limitations in the tax law reducing itemized deductions for upper-income individuals and married couples. Later on in this chapter, in Bob and Sue's case, we will see the same limitations do not apply.

Also note that in the "With the Donation" table below, "Deductions" goes from $37,636 without the donation to $97,636 with the donation. This is because of the $60,000 deduction allowable each year (30% of John and Mary's income of $200,000) for the charitable contribution of the easement.

Once again, the facts.

(1) John and Mary's income is $200,000.

(2) The income tax deduction for the easement is $1,000,000.

(3) John and Mary have $40,000 in other itemized deductions.

Without the Donation

	Years 1-6
Income	$200,000
Deductions	$37,636
Tax Due	$40,917

With the Donation

	Years 1-6
Income	$200,000
Deductions	$97,636
Tax Due	$22,059

Total tax due over six years *without* the easement donation:	$225,816
Total tax due over six years *with* the easement donation:	$132,354
Income Tax Savings:	$93,462

In addition to the income tax savings, John and Mary *have reduced their combined federal and state estate tax burden* (in most states) from $1,638,750 on a $4,000,000 estate to $1,088,750 on a $3,000,000 estate. In addition, and *this is a very important point*, any or all of the four lots they reserved under the terms of the easement can be sold, at $150,000 each, to help pay the estate tax, and *Riverview can be saved!* Finally, at their deaths, their estates may be eligible for additional tax benefits because of the conservation easement on Riverview.

Good planning? Yes! In Chapter 7, I discuss this limited development example from another point of view, and the good planning will seem even better. In addition, in Chapter 7, there is a brief discussion, and in Appendix D there is a longer discussion, of this new estate tax benefit.

Example: Bob and Sue

Bob and Sue have a current combined annual income of $40,000. Their estate, not including Diamond Farm, is worth $200,000.

They sign a conservation easement that restricts the future use of Diamond Farm to agricultural and ranching purposes; the value of Diamond Farm is reduced from $1,700,000 to $500,000.

Remember that the charitable contribution can be deducted only up to 30% of Bob and Sue's income. This means that the deduction from the easement will only be $12,000 each year (30% of $40,000). As a result, the *income tax savings* from the gift will be low.

Once again, the facts.

(1) Bob and Sue's income is $40,000.

(2) The value of the income tax deduction for the easement is $1,200,000.

(3) Assume that Bob and Sue have $6,000 in other itemized deductions.

Without the Donation

	Years 1-6
Income	$40,000
Deductions	$6,000
Tax Due	$4,170

With the Donation

	Years 1-6
Income	$40,000
Deductions	$18,000
Tax Due	$2,505

Total tax due over six years *without* the easement donation:	$25,020
Total tax due over six years *with* the easement donation:	$15,030
Income Tax Savings:	$9,990

It is important to note what Bob and Sue have been able to accomplish and what goals they have not yet been able to reach. They have achieved a modest income tax savings and a dramatic reduction in the value of their estate. But they may also want to think about reserving the same sort of *limited development rights* that were so important in John and Mary's case. By retaining the ability to create and sell a small number of lots sensibly located on the perimeter of Diamond Farm, Bob and Sue can create additional liquidity. Lots can be sold now or at a future date. Additional cash will be available to pay any estate tax that may be due. Also, at their deaths, their estates may be eligible for the estate tax benefits discussed in Appendix D. *Diamond Farm can indeed go to the children.*

(This book will not cover special federal or state estate tax programs designed to assist owners of farms or ranches. You should determine from your advisors whether such programs may be helpful for you.)

Comments and Observations

Let's be absolutely clear about what is motivating John and Mary and Bob and Sue. By restricting Riverview and Diamond Farm, they are protecting their most important asset. By preserving Riverview and Diamond Farm from development, they are also protecting their property, and their families, from the destructive impact of the estate tax.

Some family members, or some family advisors, might argue that John and Mary or Bob and Sue will be giving away a significant portion of their family's wealth. But it is very important to note that aside from achieving impor- tant family land protection goals, the "cash" difference to the family is not simply a dollar-for-dollar difference between the value of the property, unrestricted, and the value of the property after giving away the easement.

First of all, a higher-value, unrestricted Riverview or Diamond Farm will generate a *significantly larger estate tax*. Second, any income tax savings as a result of the charitable contribution may provide present dollar benefits and additional *liquid* wealth to the family that chooses to protect its land this way.

Remember: do not be fooled. If you don't *voluntarily* give up some of that high value, *on your own terms* and under a plan that you control, *in the end your family will have to pay much of that value over to Uncle Sam anyway, and on Uncle Sam's terms.*

What If....

Careful tax and conservation planning can create wonderful results for the owners *and* wonderful results for the land. What if John and Mary decide not only that they want Riverview permanently protected but also that they want Riverview to go to a conservation organization when they die?

CHAPTER 4

Gift of a Remainder Interest

Background

A *remainder interest* and a *conservation easement* are two entirely different things.

Today, John and Mary could give the local land trust the deed to Riverview, but could *reserve the right to live at Riverview until they die.* Their right to live at Riverview until they die is called a "life estate" or a "life tenancy." The act of making the gift of Riverview *now,* to *take effect at their deaths,* is called the gift of a "remainder interest."

When you donate an *easement,* you are giving away certain rights you have to do things with your property, but you are not giving up ownership of your property today or in the future and you can sell it or leave it to your children (or to anyone else) at your death. Generally, *when you donate a remainder interest, you have decided to reserve the right to live on your property until your death but your property will go to a charity when you die.*

The first way a remainder interest can qualify for an income tax deduction is by donating to *any* charitable organization a *remainder interest in a personal residence or farm.* This particular donation does not have to meet any of the "conservation purposes" tests, discussed in Chapter 3, that are important for *easement* donations. A common form that this gift takes, for example, is for a donor to give his *alma mater* a remainder interest in the donor's home. The donor continues to live on the property, and, at the donor's death, the *alma mater* sells the home and uses the proceeds in the conduct of its educational business. The simple gift of a remainder interest in a personal residence to a conservation organization or to any other charity, *without any restrictions on the future use of the property*, could qualify for an income tax deduction.

However, if John and Mary are motivated by a desire to protect Riverview, they should consider the second form of a gift of a remainder interest, the gift of a remainder interest in land "for conservation purposes." Again, this is the same "conservation purposes" test that applies to the deductible donation of conservation easements, discussed in Chapter 3. Remember that to meet the conservation purposes test the contribution truly must add to the public conservation good: preservation of important open space, significant wildlife habitat, threatened farmland or watershed, protection of historic property, and so forth. In the case of property that is the subject of a remainder gift for conservation purposes, during the landowner's "life estate" or "life tenancy" the landowner will not be able to do anything with that property that will destroy the conservation qualities to be protected by the gift.

How the Gift is Valued

If John and Mary give their children $1,000,000 today, the value of that gift is clearly $1,000,000. But what if John and Mary put that same $1,000,000 in a trust, and the terms of that trust say that John and Mary's children can't have that $1,000,000 for ten years? The *value* of the right to receive $1,000,000 in ten years is certainly less than the *value* of the right to receive $1,000,000 today.

Similarly, John and Mary can give Riverview to a charitable conservation organization *today*. The value of that gift is much greater than if John and Mary agree *now* to give Riverview to the local land trust *when they die*.

With the gift of a remainder interest, the fact that the donee organization will actually take possession of the property at some time in the future results in the value of the gift being reduced *for income tax deduction purposes*.

Let's say that John and Mary reserve the right to live at Riverview until they both die ("life estates"), and today sign a deed by which Riverview will go to the local land trust after their deaths (the gift of a "remainder interest"). Let's assume that John and Mary own Riverview jointly, that John is 65 and Mary is 62, and that Riverview is worth $2,500,000.

Based on recent IRS tables, the value of the remainder interest is $633,375. (According to the IRS tables, the discount "factor" to be used in this particular case is .25335; the value of Riverview, $2,500,000, is multiplied by the factor of .25335 to get the result of $633,375.)

As another example, if John Landowner is widowed and 65 years old, and John donates to a local conservation organization a remainder interest in Riverview for conservation purposes, the factor from the IRS tables is .39656. The value of the deduction is $991,400 (.39656 times $2,500,000).

The IRS factor has *nothing to do* with the current value of Riverview. In the previous example, if Riverview were worth $500,000 instead of $2,500,000, the factor would still be .39656 and the value of the deduction would be $198,280 (.39656 times $500,000).

As with the gift of a conservation easement or an outright gift of land, the value of the remainder interest is generally only deductible up to 30% of the donor's income, with a five-year carryforward of the balance of the deduction.

There is a Better Way

I suggest that John and Mary are missing the boat. We start with the proposition that Riverview has the characteristics (open space, scenic view, whatever) that would satisfy the "conservation purposes" test, and that John and Mary want Riverview protected. We add to that the fact that once the conservation remainder has been donated, neither John nor Mary nor any other owner of Riverview can do anything on or to Riverview that is inconsistent with the conservation gift.

Now we have an opportunity to use two different conservation and tax tools together, with good results!

I suggest that if John and Mary care about Riverview and wish to reduce their taxes they should give both a conservation easement on Riverview and a conservation remainder. They will be giving up nothing more than if the conservation remainder donation were the only gift, and the tax benefits will be considerably greater. For purposes of both the tax law and enforcement of the restrictions, I generally recommend that the easement go to one conservation organization and the remainder go to a different conservation organization. The gifts can be made at the same time or in the same year or the easement can be given in one year and the remainder interest can be given in a later year (for technical legal reasons, you may want to donate the easement first). It may even be possible to make both gifts at the same time using only one document.

Compare the tax benefits.

John Landowner is widowed and 65 years old. He gives to a charitable conservation organization an easement on Riverview, prohibiting any further development, and reduces the value of Riverview from $2,500,000 to $1,000,000. His income tax deduction is $1,500,000.

In the same year, he gives a remainder interest in Riverview (which is now restricted by the conservation easement) to a second conservation organization. The discount factor is .39656; the value of Riverview *at the time of this donation* (reduced by the easement) is $1,000,000. The income tax deduction from the remainder donation is $396,560 (.39656 times $1,000,000). The total income tax deduction is $1,896,560, compared to $991,400 with only the donation of the remainder interest. John has not really given up anything additional, since his use of Riverview is subject to the same conservation restrictions in both cases. He has just been smarter about his tax planning.

Remember, of course, as I noted in Chapter 3, *a larger income tax deduction will not always mean larger income tax savings,* because the value of the gift can generally only be deducted up to 30% of the donor's income. Obviously, each donor must review the possible results with his or her tax advisor.

A Warning

One further warning for conservation-minded land-owners who plan to give away their property, either in the form of a remainder donation or in an outright gift. *If you want your land to be protected, before you give it away, put a conservation easement on it and donate that easement to a conservation organization.*

The horror stories often go like this. Grandpa had an informal understanding with his favorite college that the college would preserve his old mansion and its beautiful gardens and use the place as an administration building. In his will, he left them the property outright, with no restrictions on its future use. Five years after Grandpa died, the college tore down the old mansion, citing pressing needs for space, and now faculty housing covers the flowerbeds. The family can do nothing.

Grandpa *could have* mixed and matched conservation giving and other charitable giving. A conservation easement donated to a charitable conservation organization would have protected the old homestead, and the property still could have been left to the college. If the college needed cash, the property could have been sold, *subject to the restrictions*, to any buyer who was willing to use the property in accordance with the terms of Grandpa's easement.

What If....

What if John and Mary don't want to get involved with all of these legal documents now? Can they simply make a gift to charity of an easement, or of Riverview, in their wills?

CHAPTER 5

A Testamentary Gift (Gift by Will)

Mother Had the Last Word

I heard a story not too long ago that may or may not be true. An elderly woman on Cape Cod, it seems, owned more than 50 acres of open and scenic property. She had summered in the big home there when she was a child and subsequently inherited the property from her parents. She had a deep love for the land and wanted to see it preserved. Her children liked what they heard from local developers, who coveted the property and made a number of offers to the elderly owner, all of which she turned down.

Finally, her children thought they won the battle. Mother had wanted to put a conservation restriction on the property, but she agreed that she would not do so during her lifetime. The children expected that when she died, they could cash in on the property's enormous value.

The children were wrong. Mother donated a conservation restriction on the property to the local land conservation organization, but she made the donation *in her will.*

You Can Make a Gift by Will

A charitable contribution of a conservation easement or an outright gift of property can be made, just like any other testamentary bequest, by will. For estate tax purposes, the full value of the gift is included in the estate and then deducted from the estate. As a *tax* matter, it is as if the property had been restricted or given away before death (and kept out of the estate at the outset). Please note, however, that any sizable charitable contribution by will *could* have other effects (in connection with the division of property under the will or the funding of certain trusts), and a careful analysis of this matter should be made for you ahead of time by an experienced estate-tax counselor. If a landowner makes a gift of a conservation easement by will, the estate is also eligible for the new estate tax benefit discussed in Chapter 7 and Appendix D.

In addition, if you plan to make a conservation gift by will, you should certainly ascertain ahead of time that the named charity will accept the gift. One way to avoid this problem (and a host of other problems that may come up in carrying out your wishes) in the case of a testamentary gift of an easement is to *include in your will specific and detailed language imposing a conservation easement, worked out with the charitable organization, to take effect at your death.*

There are advantages and disadvantages to making charitable conservation gifts by will. Unlike a lifetime gift, which for income tax purposes is generally subject to a deduction ceiling of 30% of income, a gift by will is fully deductible for estate tax purposes. On the other hand, of course, if you make a gift by will you do not get an income tax deduction, and, of course, you cannot take advantage of any income tax savings.

Finally, the gift of a conservation easement by will also makes the estate eligible for the special tax benefits discussed in Appendix D.

You May Want To Do More Than That

Unless you are planning to handle the problem like the woman at the Cape, and if you are certain that you want to protect your land by making a conservation gift, you have a great deal to gain by making that gift while you are alive, *and making the most out of any income tax deductions*, rather than making a gift by will. Obviously, if you are not certain about what you want to do, revising your will to include a conservation gift (either an easement or an outright gift of the property) can give you estate tax "protection" while at the same time preserving your right to change your mind. Comprehensive planning can also include gifts at death through the use of *trusts created during the donor's lifetime*; this is often a flexible and desirable technique and you should discuss it with your advisors.

A landowner who fully intends to leave land outright to a conservation organization at his or her death should remember that the current gift of a remainder interest to a charitable organization will generate income tax deductions that can produce tax savings. Further, as I indicated in Chapter 4 on remainder interests, once you have decided to donate a remainder interest for conservation purposes there is another important step you can take. You possibly can create further tax benefits without giving up any additional rights by donating an easement on the property before you donate the remainder interest.

What If....

What if John and Mary aren't so charitably inclined this year, but are still sensitive to the estate tax burden Riverview will generate? Can't they just give the property to their children?

CHAPTER 6

Giving to Other Family Members Now

It Won't Work This Way

"Why should I worry about the estate tax?" John Landowner asks. "We'll just sign the property over to the children, and Mary and I will stay here as long as we want."

This is something that I hear from time to time and every time I do it makes me cringe.

This is not as simple or as painless as it sounds. Not only that, "signing the property over to the children" may give John and Mary a false sense of security, and as a result they may not take *similar* tax-planning steps that *do work*.

The Rules

In order to know what is wrong with John and Mary's idea, there are a few tax rules we need to understand about gifts to other family members while you are alive (sometimes called "lifetime giving").

First, if you give away property to someone other than your spouse, but *retain the right to use or enjoy that property, the value of the property (the property you thought you had given away) will be included in your estate at your death.* It is important to recognize the significance of this rule. If John and Mary "give away" Riverview, for example, to their children, but if they continue to live at Riverview and use the property and enjoy it, the full value of Riverview will be included in their estates when they die.

Why is this so? In part, this is because the tax law takes the position that if John and Mary retain the right to continue to use and enjoy Riverview, they haven't truly given Riverview away. In fact, the IRS would argue, the only reason John and Mary signed Riverview over to the children was to try to avoid the estate tax.

Now, note that if John and Mary signed Riverview over to the children and moved into a place in town, the results would be quite different. Under those circumstances, the value of Riverview would not be included in their estates when they die. But the gift of Riverview to the children now would be a *taxable gift.*

"What!?" you say. "Do you mean that if I just deed my house over to my children and move out I have to pay a tax?"

The answer is, it depends (that sounds just like a lawyer). *The second tax rule that is important for this chapter* is that you can generally give away up to $10,000 a year ($20,000 if spouses join in the gift; check with your advisor for details) to as many different people as you would like without any gift tax liability. If you want to give away property *faster* than that, *you may have to pay a gift tax.* Whether or not John and Mary will actually have to pay a gift tax on the gift of Riverview to the children will depend, among other things, on how much Riverview is worth and on whether or not they have made other gifts, this year or in prior years, above the $10,000 per person ceiling.

The third tax rule that is important for this chapter is that spouses can make unlimited gifts to each other, while they are alive or at death (by will), without any federal gift tax or estate tax. Cash, stocks, land, anything, it generally doesn't matter for federal gift tax or estate tax purposes as long as the transfer is from one spouse to another.

The fourth tax rule that is important for this chapter is this. In addition to allowing individuals to make annual $10,000 gifts (again, $20,000 if spouses give together), and in addition to allowing spouses to make unlimited gifts to each other, the federal tax law generally allows each individual to transfer to others more than $600,000 worth of property (cash, stocks, land, *any* property), during lifetime or at death, without paying any federal estate tax or gift tax. (For many years this amount was $600,000; Congress changed the law in 1997. In 1998 the amount is

$625,000, and by the year 2006 this number increases, in gradual steps, to $1,000,000. See the Estate Tax Tables at Appendix B.)

What does all this mean? *If you want to give valuable property to your family while you are alive, before you do you must consult a tax attorney.*

Done Right, Lifetime Giving Might Make Sense

Giving Riverview to the children now, even if John and Mary have to pay a gift tax, may turn out to be a smart thing to do.

For example, if Riverview is worth $500,000 now and increases in value at a rate of 7% a year, in 10 years the value of Riverview will have almost doubled. The property will then be a million-dollar asset for John and Mary to contend with in their estates. On the other hand, if John and Mary give Riverview to their children now (of course, assuming that they can afford to and assuming that it otherwise makes good sense), the future increase in value of Riverview will not be taxed as part of their estates.

There are other lifetime giving techniques that John and Mary should consider.

For example, if Riverview is worth $500,000, and if John and Mary have two married children, they can give each child and each child's spouse $20,000 "worth" of

Riverview each year. The best way to set up this sort of family giving program will vary from family to family and from state to state. Your professional advisor will be able to help you on this point. In five years, they would be able to give away $400,000 of the "value" of Riverview (although if Riverview continues to increase, it may take longer than John and Mary think to give away all of Riverview this way). One potential risk that John and Mary run, of course, is that if the long-term preservation of Riverview is important to them, without careful planning this annual giving may be wonderful for estate tax purposes but the children (bless them) may one day sell out or divorce.

This leads to a further planning possibility. John and Mary could put a conservation restriction on Riverview, reducing its value, generating an income tax deduction, and permanently protecting it. Then John and Mary could begin a program of annual family gifts, in the end giving away Riverview in a shorter period of time.

If John and Mary have enough other assets and are the kind of people who for tax and family reasons make annual gifts to their children and possibly their grand-children, giving the family Riverview may be preferable to giving the family cash. As I noted earlier, if Riverview continues to appreciate, getting it (and the potential future appreciation) out of their estates early may be a sensible thing to do.

Other Techniques

There are a variety of other, more specialized wealth-transfer techniques, including the use of trusts that can run for many generations, life insurance, and charitable trusts, that I have not covered here. (See in Chapter 9 the brief discussion about *Preserving Family Lands: Book II – More Planning Strategies for the Future*.) Further, the estate tax consequences of any family gift program should be thoroughly reviewed in light of special federal estate tax valuation rules. Once again, however, this book is only designed to provide an introduction to some of the tax issues and techniques involved in family land preservation. A good advisor should be able to provide you with a more extensive menu, and can help you integrate estate-planning techniques with current family needs.

CHAPTER 7

Cash Sale Compared to Good Planning

Thanks, But We'll Take the Cash

"We're glad you have taken the time to share this all with us," John and Mary might now say. "But we think we'll take the money."

What does the Landowner family end up with if John and Mary sell Riverview now, while prices are high? *Much less than they think.*

If the sale price is $2,500,000, and the cost of Riverview was $100,000, they have $2,400,000 of gain; the federal income tax on the gain is $475,880 (without taking into consideration any special federal income tax benefits that might be available to John and Mary on the sale of their principal residence). Assume John and Mary live in Massachusetts; the Massachusetts tax on the gain is $72,000. John and Mary now take the after-tax proceeds of the sale, $1,952,120, and invest that money in tax-free municipals. (For these calculations we will not include any income on the municipals.)

Mary dies first, leaving everything to John. When John dies, assume he leaves $1,500,000 in other assets, and the municipals, to the children:

- The federal estate tax on the $3,452,120 estate is $1,112,812. The estate tax in Massachusetts (and most other states) is $224,604. Total tax due? $1,337,416!!! (Again, see the Estate Tax Tables at Appendix B.)

- *More than half of the proceeds from the sale of Riverview are almost gone.* Outrageous? Confiscatory? Poor planning? True!!

- *Riverview is gone.* Eighty houses and a small park cover the once-loved site.

- After paying estate taxes, the Landowner family has $2,114,704 left.

Is This a Better Idea?

Now, compare this awful result with the limited development possibility we discussed in Chapter 3. Remember that John and Mary put a conservation easement on Riverview but reserved the right to keep their house and large lot and to create four additional house lots on Riverview. The value of Riverview was reduced to $1,500,000; the deduction was $1,000,000; the income tax savings from the easement donation was $93,462.

Assume the Landowners hold Riverview until they die. The estate of the survivor, consisting of $1,500,000 plus Riverview (to keep it simple we will assume no increase in the value of Riverview), is taxed as follows:

■ The federal estate tax on the $3,000,000 estate is $906,750. The Massachusetts estate tax is $182,000. Total estate tax? $1,088,750.

■ The four "reserved" lots on Riverview can be sold, at $150,000 each, to help pay the estate tax. Because the Landowners held their land until they died, there will be no (or very little) tax to pay on the proceeds of these sales. (See below for an explanation of this point.)

■ If John and Mary's heirs don't want to keep Riverview, it can be sold (again, with little or no tax to pay), but *Riverview will forever be protected.*

■ After paying estate taxes, the Landowner family has $1,911,250 left, *including Riverview.* If we add to that the $93,462 income tax savings from the easement donation, *the dollar difference between selling out and holding on has virtually disappeared and John and Mary have left more value to their children by preserving Riverview.*

■ This is good planning!

The same limited development possibilities also work well for the family that has current cash needs. Under such circumstances, John and Mary could consider the possibility of protecting Riverview with a conservation easement reserving limited development rights, and then selling one or more lots. With proper planning, the charitable contribution deduction can be used against a portion of the gain from the sale of the lots. Your advisors can help you with this planning.

As I mentioned above, because John and Mary held Riverview until they died, if the house lots are sold shortly after their deaths there will be little or no tax to pay on the proceeds of the sales. This is because of an important tax rule. When an individual dies owning property (stocks, land, *any* kind of property), the "basis" (generally speaking, the *cost*) of that property is increased (or "stepped up") *for income tax purposes* to whatever the *value* of that property was at the death of the owner. In other words, in the above example, if the *value* of each of the reserved lots was $150,000 after the deaths of John and Mary, and those lots were subsequently *sold* for $150,000 each, there would be *no gain for income tax purposes*, which means, of course, that no income tax would be due because of the sale.

For many property owners, the *dollar* comparison between selling and preserving (with limited development) will not be as close as it is in John and Mary's case, above.

But the point is clear. You do have choices.

This Is Good Enough But There Is More

If we stop here we can already see how by doing the planning John and Mary can make some sensible choices. However, there are very important additional estate tax benefits that need to be considered. These benefits are covered in greater detail in Appendix D.

In 1997 Congress added to the tax law an additional incentive for landowners who protect their land with conservation easements. Very simply, this new benefit (called Section 2031(c) of the tax code) allows an executor to exclude from the taxable estate an additional 40% of the value of land subject to a conservation easement, *in addition to any decrease in value already attributable to the restrictions imposed by the easement.* This exclusion is available assuming the situation meets all of the relevant requirements of the new rule and is subject to all of the limitations of the new rule; again, these are discussed in greater detail in Appendix D.

Here is the simplest possible example of how this new benefit works. Assume Mary owns land worth $2,000,000. She donates an easement that lowers the value of the land to $1,000,000. She dies, and assume the land is still worth $1,000,000. *An additional 40% of the value of that land, or*

an additional $400,000, can be excluded from her tax-
able estate, so the land value subject to estate tax is
$600,000!!

Now let's look again at the example we have covered
in this chapter. John and Mary have already reduced the
value of Riverview with a conservation easement and
reduced the estate tax at John's death. Using the benefits
of this new incentive, John's executor could potentially
reduce John's taxable estate by up to an additional
$500,000, for an additional estate tax savings of more than
$200,000!! In fact, *with good planning from the beginning,*
it may even be possible for *both* Mary's estate and John's
estate to take advantage of this new incentive, with potentially twice the estate tax savings!!

Is There a Message Here?

Yes!!

Don't assume that any particular plan or approach
will produce the best after-tax dollar results. Run the
numbers!!

What's Next?

A general understanding of how to use the various tax
incentives for land conservation to generate income tax
savings and estate tax savings is only one piece of the
family land planning puzzle. Who else should the

Farmowners talk to? What else do the Landowners need to know to start?

Preserving Family Lands

CHAPTER 8

Sources of Help and Other Issues

What Do I Give Up? And What Do I Keep?

It shouldn't be too difficult to figure out the income tax and estate tax benefits from a gift of land or a conservation easement. It may be more difficult to reach agreement among family members about what (if anything) should be done with the family's land (if in fact the owner or owners of the land seek input from other family members).

For some families, the land may be their single most valuable asset; reducing or restricting its value may simply be unaffordable. In other families, significant land with important conservation qualities may be only a small piece of wealth compared to other family assets, but inertia may outweigh social conscience and financial planning and the land will go on the auction block.

Then there are those families willing to forego some value (even if it hurts a little) for the sake of preserving an irreplaceable asset. For these people, agreement on a family land conservation plan that takes into consideration current and future financial and conservation goals may be easy to arrive at or it may be the product of extensive debates and even loud arguments.

It will be helpful for these people to know that, in most cases, once a landowner has made the choice to preserve his or her property, there may be a range of ways to do that. For example, as Chapter 7 illustrates, with a property of any considerable size, the ability to do some additional limited development while preserving *almost* all of the property's conservation values may provide the necessary flexibility to protect the property while still retaining much of its value.

In addition, the state of the art of land planning and tax and legal planning for landowners is becoming better each year. With the help of a knowledgeable advisor who can provide the family with a wide range of choices, the family that is willing to work together can almost always resolve a "preserve it/sell it" dispute. If you are in the middle of such a dispute, or if you think you might be when some of your family members find out you are reading this book, the "resource people" identified below should be able to help you sort out and evaluate the various options that may be available to you.

Recipient of the Gift

For the gift to be eligible for an income tax deduction, a charitable conservation organization or a unit of government must agree to hold the easement (or the property). In some limited situations, a charity that is not primarily conservation-oriented may be an eligible donee for a conservation easement, but this is the exception rather than the rule.

Obviously, at some early point in their planning the Landowners will have to identify a donee for their gift. Many land trusts around the country have well-informed staff or volunteers who can provide invaluable technical assistance and advice to a potential donor, including names of land planning, legal, and other professional advisors who may be an integral part of the process. Many land conservation organizations will also have literature that will be helpful to you in your planning.

If you don't know where to begin asking about a donee organization, you can start anywhere from a local land trust to a local conservation commission to a State Game and Fish Department (throughout this book, references to "conservation organizations" mean both private charitable organizations and state or local governmental conservation agencies). If there is a local land trust in your area, the people from that organization will most certainly give you a warm welcome.

Some national conservation organizations, such as The Nature Conservancy, the Trust for Public Land, the Audubon Society, or the American Farmland Trust, have regional or even state offices. The staff people will be very knowledgeable about who in your particular area might be a logical choice as a donee. In recent years, a wider range of national organizations, such as Ducks Unlimited and the Rocky Mountain Elk Foundation, have also begun accepting easements.

The Land Trust Alliance, with a national office at 1319 F Street, N.W., Suite 501, Washington, DC 20004-1106 (phone: 202-638-4725; fax: 202-638-4730), can help you identify local land trusts and other conservation organizations and can also provide you with background literature. A Land Trust Alliance publication, "The Conservation Easement Handbook" (a joint project with the Trust for Public Land), includes much useful material. Another Land Trust Alliance publication, "Appraising Easements" (a joint project with the National Trust for Historic Preservation), should be helpful for your appraiser.

Legal Advice, Including Tax

The donation of land to charity should not be done without the advice of an attorney who is experienced in this specialty or willing to affiliate with someone who is. An outright gift of land is generally a simple matter; the gift of a conservation easement or remainder interest is not; and all of these gifts involve significant tax consequences.

"Of course he's going to say that," you think. "He's a tax lawyer." *Anyone who tells you this task can be undertaken without competent tax and other legal advice doesn't understand the seriousness of what is being accomplished.* If you give away your property, it's gone, forever. If you record a conservation easement on your property, you have not only forever restricted your ability to do with it what you please, you have also given some outside organization the authority to enforce those restrictions. Now, in many cases these are truly fine and wonderful things to do, but if you do them you should do them right.

Your lawyer should do them right, too. If you find a lawyer to do this work for you, *ask the lawyer how many times he or she has done this sort of thing before.* If you don't know where to turn, local land conservation organizations ought to be able to help you find good, experienced legal help; your donee organization may be a good place to start.

Remember that in addition to understanding the law of conservation easements, *your tax advisor must also be sensitive to all the related tax and legal planning that should be done in connection with your gift.*

This book does *not* consider the tax consequences of a bargain sale. In a bargain sale, the owner *sells* an asset to a charitable organization for less than its current value;

the sale generates for the seller *both* taxable gain and a charitable contribution deduction. Many tax-exempt charitable organizations do not have sufficient funds to participate in a bargain sale. If the charity you identify can pay you, your advisors should be able to help you determine the tax consequences.

The cost of legal advice will vary with the complexity of the donation. In the case of an outright gift of property, the fee for preparing a deed usually will be nominal if no subdivision is involved. In a simple easement case, with one donor and very limited reserved rights, the fee for drafting a conservation easement should be *relatively* low. The legal costs begin to grow as more parties become involved and, for example, as the landowner and his or her lawyer begin to negotiate with the charity over the extent of the reserved rights. In addition, costs go up when the landowner wants the lawyer to do most of the negotiating.

As a general rule, in a *very simple case* the legal fees for a conservation easement could be $5,000 or less, not including any possible fees for travel time. Depending on the complexity of the work the cost could be significantly higher. In many cases I am aware of, when several family members had the opportunity to review, disagree about, and comment on numerous easement drafts, the legal fees were well in excess of $20,000.

For many landowners and many families, a conservation easement should be only one part of a larger family land planning, estate planning, and asset planning project. *Do not be "penny wise and pound foolish." Comprehensive and successful planning is not inexpensive, but comprehensive and successful planning for families that own land is an important and intelligent investment for current and future generations.* I discuss this point in a little greater detail in the next chapter and in much greater detail in *Preserving Family Lands: Book II – More Planning Strategies for the Future.*

Appraiser

You must hire an appraiser.

Under the tax law, any person who makes a charitable contribution of property with a claimed value in excess of $5,000 must have a "qualified appraisal" or the tax deduction for the gift may be disallowed.

A "qualified appraisal" must include, among other things, a description of the property, the method used to determine its value, information about the appraiser's qualifications, and a description of the fee arrangement between the donor and the appraiser.

Once again, in addition to the practical requirement

that an appraiser be hired, the earlier a donor has an idea of what the value of the contribution will be, the more opportunity will exist for any tax planning that might be advisable in the year of the gift. For a donor who is considering reserving some future development rights, an early valuation review of the different possibilities is a good idea.

The cost of an appraisal may run from $500 for the simplest house appraisal to more than $10,000 for a complex appraisal of a high-value easement.

The value of a good appraisal cannot be emphasized too much: in an audit with the IRS, the qualifications of the appraiser and the thoroughness of the appraisal can be very important factors.

Land Planner or Consultant

A land planner or consultant can help you review different limited development possibilities for your land.

There are a number of situations in which such an advisor will *not* be necessary. A donor who is not going to reserve any future development rights will not need a land planner. A donor with a very large tract of land who wants to reserve the right to carve out a few house lots *may* not require such services. Additionally, the need for the preparation and even possible recording of a plan preserving future development rights will vary widely from state to state. Your legal advisor can help you determine whether a land planner is necessary.

In some situations, as I noted in Chapter 3, *any* further development will simply be incompatible with conservation goals. Also, in some situations, the reservation of too many future development rights may also threaten a landowner's claim to an income tax deduction for the donation of a conservation easement. In other situations, however, it may be possible, through sensitive location of house sites and with a minimum of intrusion, to do limited future building on restricted property.

A land planner who is sensitive both to environmental and open space concerns and to the tax law's requirements for the deductibility of an easement donation can help. Such planners can often bring to a project not just sensitive and practical planning techniques but also appraisal capabilities.

If you need such a person, the same sources of information referred to above (land trusts and other charitable conservation organizations, etc.) should be able to point you in the right direction. Make sure you have some confirmation that any person you retain has done this sort of work before.

The cost of a land planner or consultant will generally run from $5,000 to $20,000, depending on the size of your parcel, the number of limited development options to be considered, and the complexity of the situation. This is a fair price to pay for proper management of an illiquid asset. In fact, a fee in this range for a comprehensive review of development/conservation options on a $2,000,000 piece of property compares favorably with the usual fees for proper management of a comparably-valued securities portfolio, especially when you consider that a sensible limited development plan, when implemented, will often result in major income and estate tax savings.

Surveyor

You may need a survey to clarify the boundaries of your property. Sometimes the donee organization, such as a land trust, may require a current survey. Ask your legal advisor or consultant what the price range should be in your state for a survey of your property. Keep two things in mind. First, survey work need only be done after you have made the final decision about what to do with your land. Second, it may take months to secure the services of a qualified surveyor and to have the job completed.

Deductibility

Many of the costs and fees discussed above are deductible in figuring your federal income tax to the extent they exceed, when added to certain other miscellaneous itemized deductions, 2% of your adjusted gross income. Note that this is *not* the same as the deduction for the charitable contribution itself.

Property Taxes

The gift of a conservation restriction on land will reduce the value of that land, often considerably. If you donate a conservation restriction on your property, it would stand to reason that your property tax should drop. Unfortunately, I understand that many local assessors are not immediately responsive to the drop in value of restricted property, and some conservation-minded donors may end up fighting city hall over this matter.

Your attorney will be able to help you with the planning on this issue, should that become necessary. There are court decisions that state that when the value of property is reduced by a conservation restriction, the property tax assessment should generally drop to reflect the restrictions.

In addition, many states and municipalities have special assessment programs for property where the use is restricted to farmland, forestland, or open space. Your advisors can help you determine whether your property is eligible for any of these programs.

Timing

One particular lesson I have learned through the course of my work in this field is that it always takes longer than expected to do all the necessary work and complete the gift of a conservation restriction. If a landowner wants to complete a conservation gift in a particular year, tax planning and planning for the gift should begin *as early in the year as possible.* In some cases, the work can be done quickly, but a donor should not count on that happening. Sometimes when a survey is required it turns out that no qualified local surveyor can *begin* the work for months, let alone deliver a finished product in time.

If different generations within a family are asked to participate, the planning process can be a lengthy one. Giving away land or restricting its use means giving up wealth, and no matter what the social (or even the tax) benefits, some family members may be opposed. Difficult non-tax issues often come up when many family members own (or expect to own) the same land together; guidance from an experienced legal advisor and early planning are essential in these situations.

A successful compromise, if one can be reached, will often involve keeping some significant value, and potential liquidity, by reserving limited development rights. With a large tract of land the variations on this theme can be endless. The message is simple: allow adequate time for planning.

Comments and Observations

The charitable gift of land or of a conservation easement can involve a lot of work, a lot of planning (much of which your advisors can do for you), possibly a lot of decisions, and some expense. In many cases, the income tax savings from the charitable deduction can help "recover" much of the out-of-pocket expense, and this certainly underscores the value of good tax planning. However, in a much broader sense, for the landowners with whom I have worked, the deep satisfaction of permanently preserving their own land far outweighs any of the short-term work and costs.

Preserving Family Lands

CHAPTER 9

Three Problems and a Solution

If you care about open space in this country today, if you care about wildlife habitat, productive farmland, ranchland, and forestland, or if you want to preserve a way of life, you need to know that this country is facing three major problems when it comes to the protection of important privately-owned land.

The first problem is the federal estate tax, and by now readers should understand that. I've said it before and I'll repeat it here: for the first time in the history of the United States, the family that just wants to leave its land to the children may not be able to do that any more. The land may have become so valuable it may have to be sold to pay the estate tax. John and Mary and Riverview and Bob and Sue and Diamond Farm are good examples of what I mean.

Here is the second problem. A number of years ago I attended a national conference in Montana, and a speaker from Montana had this to say.

"There are 90 million acres of land in Montana," he said, "and over the next fifteen to twenty years 30 million of those acres are going to change hands. That's because that's how much land we have that is owned by people who are an average age of 59 1/2."

That is really remarkable, I thought. And then I thought, you know, that's true not only in Montana, it's also true in Virginia...and New York...and Florida...and Colorado...and *all over the United States.* The principal private landowners in this country are older, 55 and older, even 65 and older. And over the next fifteen to twenty years, millions and millions of acres around the country are going to change hands, and potentially change use, as these older landowners plan for, or don't plan for, what's going to happen to their land.

The principal private landowners in this country are older. In New England, the average age of the woodlot owner is well over 60. In the Southeast, the average age of the private forestland owner is almost 70. I was told recently that one-third of the forestland owners in Oregon are over 75!! When you combine the threat of the estate tax with the demographics of this country, it becomes absolutely clear that millions and millions of acres of open space, wildlife habitat, farmland, forestland, wildlife corridors, watershed, and ranchland *are at risk over the next few decades.*

The third problem is what I call the "good help is hard to get" problem.

In every single community in this country, if you have a piece of land that you want to *develop*, an entire infrastructure exists to support you. There are attorneys, engineers, land use planners, surveyors, appraisers, and planning board or zoning commission members who know all about how to develop a piece of land. There is a whole support network of professionals and technicians who make a living doing real estate development. If you have a piece of land to develop, the question isn't, "How can I find help?" If you have a piece of land to develop, the question is, "Let's see, of all of the available choices, who shall I choose to help me and to work with me?"

But consider this. In every single community in this country there are landowners who love their land and don't want to see that land developed. And most of them have *absolutely nowhere to turn.* In most communities around the country there are absolutely no professionals who understand how to protect a piece of land. In most communities around the country there are no attorneys, no accountants, no "planners," no zoning commission members, no appraisers, no real estate brokers, no advisors at all who understand the concept of private land protection and how to go about that.

On one hand, we have a real estate development infrastructure permanently in place and highly visible after two hundred years of real estate development in this country. On the other hand, a landowner with a farm, a ranch, working forestland, country property, and open space, has absolutely no idea where to turn for help.

This must change.

Consider this. What if instead of owning Riverview John and Mary had a successful family business? Would John and Mary and their advisors have done some sophisticated tax, financial, and legal planning to get the family business through the transfer tax system to the children??? It's likely that there would be a shareholder agreement, buy-sell provisions for the stock, life insurance, a program of annual gifts of stock, and perhaps a stock recapitalization. In short, there is a whole array of entirely appropriate tools to keep that business intact and get it to the kids.

Why haven't John and Mary and their advisors done the same sort of sophisticated, aggressive, creative planning for Riverview??? Why haven't Bob and Sue done the planning for Diamond Farm? "Succession planning for the business owner" is an accepted tax planning and financial planning discipline. For those of us who value open space, wildlife habitat, farmland, forestland, and ranchland, and the outdoor recreational opportunities that come with open land, *I think it's time we begin to focus on tax, legal, and financial planning for family lands. It's time we begin to focus on "succession planning for the landowner."*

That's why I wrote *Preserving Family Lands: Book II.* That book is not an "update" of this book, or a "revision." That book is the next book in the series, the book that introduces landowners and their advisors to a number of other planning techniques that can be used to help the family realize its goal of keeping the family's land intact.

The principal tool in the private landowner's toolbox is the conservation easement, but it is not the only tool. A planning strategy may include the use of a family limited partnership, a "generation-skipping trust," and possibly annual gifts to children and grandchildren. Often, too, more sophisticated planning involves the use of other forms of tax-advantaged charitable giving, including various forms of charitable trusts and family private foundations.

Preserving Family Lands: Book II covers a number of these subjects, and if you are interested in doing this planning, if you understand that "preserving family lands" means more than just conservation easements, I urge you to read "Book II." (There is an order form inside the back cover of *this* book.)

The purpose of this chapter is not to explain these tools. The purpose here is to make three points.

First, open space is threatened because of an aging population of landowners and the impact of high federal estate taxes.

Second, this is a problem that landowners can do something about.

Third, this is a problem that needs attention now. Awareness of these issues should force landowners to act, to do the planning, and to protect and preserve the open space that is so important to all of us.

CHAPTER 10

What Do I Do Now?

You know now (in fact, you knew before you opened this book) that you want to do something to protect your land. You may have discussed this matter with your family. You are ready to move ahead. But you need more information and you need more help.

Where is the best place to start?

If you ask a person from a local land conservation organization where to begin, he or she is likely to say, "Start with us. We can help you through the decision-making process and we can identify other good resource people and professionals if you need them."

If you ask a land planning consultant with experience in this specialty where to begin the answer will probably be, "Start with me. I know what I need to know to get you through the process. I can coordinate everything."

An attorney who has done land conservation work would reply to your question, "Let's begin now. I can provide you with a checklist of the things you need to do and we can talk about the decisions you have to make."

Who is right? They all are. This is a narrow enough area of life and law so that once you step inside it and make the decision to go ahead, any of these specialists can help you begin to put things together.

Please note this, however. *We are talking about a specialized area of family and financial planning.* You should not ask a brilliant personal injury lawyer to handle the probate of your mother's estate and you should not ask a tax lawyer to defend a client against a drunken driving charge. Similarly, it is a rare family counselor who knows how to solve the family's land planning problems and complete the family's land planning project. *If necessary, a specialist should be retained to work with the family's lawyer on this particular matter.*

If you still don't know where to begin, find a city or town official who is knowledgeable about land conservation and environmental protection and get a few names of qualified professionals or state or local charitable land trusts or other conservation organizations. One or two telephone calls should put you in touch with the right person or people. If the person you are talking to does not understand what you want to do, you have not yet found the right person. You will know when you have found the right people because *they will understand exactly what you are talking about* and they will be very glad to hear from you.

Your desire to protect and preserve your land and to confront your estate-tax problem has taken you this far. Re-read Chapter 1 and remember, *doing nothing about your land can have awful consequences.* So don't stop now, and good luck.

Stephen J. Small
Boston, Massachusetts
August, 1998

APPENDIX A

The Landowner's Quiz

What do you think the combined federal and state estate tax would be on your estate?

1. My net worth, <u>not including</u> the value of my real estate, is _____.

2. The value of my real estate is _____.

3. Therefore, the total value of my estate is _____.

4. If my estate were fully taxable, the combined federal and state estate tax would be _____.

5. In order to pay this tax, my heirs will have to

_____

_____

_____.

DON'T LOOK AT THE ESTATE TAX TABLES IN
APPENDIX B UNTIL YOU HAVE COMPLETED THIS PAGE

Appendix B

Estate Tax Tables
Total Federal and State Estate Tax Due at Death

Comments and Observations

The Estate Tax Tables that follow show the different levels of estate tax due, in all 50 states and the District of Columbia, based on rates and information available in 1998.

As noted in Chapter 6, prior to 1998 any individual could leave an estate of up to $600,000 without paying any estate tax. Congress changed the law in 1997, so the $600,000 threshold increases in gradual steps to $1,000,000 by the year 2006. Tables 1, 2, and 3 show the estate tax for every state for 1998 and also include taxes due for certain estates in the years 2000 and 2006, as the new rules are phased in.

Under the laws of some states, there may be variations that could change the results in the tables. To keep the tables as simple as possible, I have assumed that those variations do not apply. *You must check with your advisor to determine how the estate tax rules in your own state will affect your own particular situation and your family's situation.* Some states, for example, have an *inheritance* tax instead of an *estate* tax. The *effect* is the same: the total dollar amount due, shown in the tables, must be paid to the federal and state government.

In addition, as with federal and state *income* tax rates and rules, federal and state *estate* tax rates and rules can change. In some states, *gift taxes* are significant. *Check with your advisor about the rates and rules in your own state.* (Note that even with some variations from state to state, the overall results are fairly close among almost all states.)

All this having been said, however, the tables make absolutely clear the *enormous impact* of estate taxes. Note that in many states (such as Florida, for example) popularly thought to be "havens" from high estate taxes, significant federal and state estate taxes can be due once the taxable estate exceeds $625,000. In 1998, on a $2,000,000 taxable estate, *in every state, no less than $578,750 is due in taxes.* In the year 2000, on a $2,500,000 taxable estate, *in every state, no less than $805,250 is due in taxes.* By the year 2006, when you can pass $1,000,000 to your heirs without any estate tax, on a $5,000,000 taxable estate, in every state, *no less than $2,045,000 is still due in taxes.*

Because of the new rules, many readers might think,

"Well, this is quite a break, so now I don't need to do any planning."

I disagree!

First, if you are a landowner, it is certainly not unreasonable to expect that *the value of your land (and possibly your other assets) will increase* as the years go by.

Second, depending on the size of your estate, even though your estate tax bill may be less in 2006 than it will be in 1998, with larger estates *a sizable estate tax will still be due.* For example, in most states the total estate tax on a $5,000,000 estate is $2,170,250 in 1998 and $2,045,000 in 2006. This is a savings of more than $120,000 but the tax bill is still over $2,000,000!! Note that Table 4 illustrates this point in greater detail. Again, while the estate tax on a $1,000,000 estate drops to 0 by the year 2006, on larger estates the tax is still high.

Third, it's simply a mistake to put off the planning.

Preserving Family Lands

Table 1

Total federal and state estate tax due in 1998 in every state on taxable estates of various dollar amounts

Amount Of Your Taxable Estate:	$625,000	$1,000,000	$2,000,000	$2,500,000	$5,000,000	$10,000,000
Estate Tax Due By State:						
Most States[1]	0	143,750	578,750	823,750	2,188,750	4,938,750
Connecticut	11,083	159,170	642,170	905,170	2,303,370	4,949,370
Delaware	30,500	163,550	592,150	827,950	2,188,750	4,938,750
Indiana	20,750	155,800	611,400	867,200	2,229,400	4,938,750
Kansas	23,000	146,773	578,750	823,750	2,188,750	4,938,750
Kentucky	15,000	143,750	578,750	823,750	2,188,750	4,938,750
Louisiana	17,800	143,750	578,750	823,750	2,188,750	4,938,750
Maryland	6,250	143,750	578,750	823,750	2,188,750	4,938,750
Mississippi	250	143,750	578,750	823,750	2,188,750	4,938,750
Nebraska	6,150	143,750	578,750	823,750	2,188,750	4,938,750

Table 1 (continued)

Total federal and state estate tax due in 1998 in every state on taxable estates of various dollar amounts

Amount Of Your Taxable Estate:	$625,000	$1,000,000	$2,000,000	$2,500,000	$5,000,000	$10,000,000
Estate Tax Due By State:						
New York	27,000	164,050	625,650	885,450	2,338,650	5,307,650
North Carolina	1,750	143,750	592,150	847,950	2,255,150	4,938,750
Ohio	31,850	168,650	607,250	848,050	2,188,750	4,938,750
Oklahoma	19,350	156,275	604,000	849,800	2,188,750	4,938,750
Pennsylvania	37,500	170,550	599,150	834,950	2,188,750	4,938,750
South Dakota	43,125	181,800	625,400	868,700	2,188,750	4,938,750
Tennessee	1,375	143,750	600,550	853,850	2,203,550	4,938,750

[1]Alabama, Alaska, Arizona, Arkansas, California, Colorado, District of Columbia, Florida, Georgia, Hawaii, Idaho, Illinois, Iowa, Maine, Massachusetts, Michigan, Minnesota, Missouri, Montana, Nevada, New Hampshire, New Jersey, New Mexico, North Dakota, Oregon, Rhode Island, South Carolina, Texas, Utah, Vermont, Virginia, Washington, West Virginia, Wisconsin, Wyoming

Table 2
Total federal and state estate tax due in 2000 in every state on taxable estates of various dollar amounts

Amount Of Your Taxable Estate:	$1,000,000	$2,500,000	$5,000,000
Estate Tax Due By State:			
Most States[1]	125,250	805,250	2,170,250
Delaware	145,050	809,450	2,170,250
Indiana	137,300	848,700	2,210,900
Kansas	129,198	805,250	2,170,250
New York	145,550	866,950	2,320,150
North Carolina	125,250	829,450	2,236,650
Ohio	150,150	829,550	2,170,250
Oklahoma	137,775	831,300	2,170,250
Pennsylvania	152,050	816,450	2,170,250
South Dakota	163,300	850,200	2,170,250
Tennessee	125,250	835,350	2,185,050

[1]Alabama, Alaska, Arizona, Arkansas, California, Colorado, Connecticut, District of Columbia, Florida, Georgia, Hawaii, Idaho, Illinois, Iowa, Kentucky, Louisiana, Maine, Maryland, Massachusetts, Michigan, Minnesota, Mississippi, Missouri, Montana, Nebraska, Nevada, New Hampshire, New Jersey, New Mexico, North Dakota, Oregon, Rhode Island, South Carolina, Texas, Utah, Vermont, Virginia, Washington, West Virginia, Wisconsin, Wyoming

Table 3
Total federal and state estate tax due in 2006 in every state on taxable estates of various dollar amounts

Amount Of Your Taxable Estate:	$1,000,000	$2,500,000	$5,000,000
Estate Tax Due By State:			
Most States[1]	0	680,000	2,045,000
Delaware	53,000	684,200	2,045,000
Indiana	45,250	723,450	2,085,650
Kansas	41,750	680,000	2,045,000
Maryland	10,000	680,000	2,045,000
Mississippi	10,040	680,000	2,045,000
Nebraska	9,900	680,000	2,045,000
North Carolina	28,000	704,200	2,111,400
Ohio	58,100	704,300	2,045,000
Oklahoma	45,725	706,050	2,045,000
Pennsylvania	60,000	691,200	2,045,000
South Dakota	71,250	724,950	2,045,000
Tennessee	27,200	710,100	2,059,800

[1]Alabama, Alaska, Arizona, Arkansas, California, Colorado, Connecticut, District of Columbia, Florida, Georgia, Hawaii, Idaho, Illinois, Iowa, Kentucky, Louisiana, Maine, Massachusetts, Michigan, Minnesota, Missouri, Montana, Nevada, New Hampshire, New Jersey, New Mexico, New York, North Dakota, Oregon, Rhode Island, South Carolina, Texas, Utah, Vermont, Virginia, Washington, West Virginia, Wisconsin, Wyoming

Table 4

Total federal and state estate tax due in "Most States" on taxable estates of various dollar amounts in 1998, 2000, and 2006

Amount Of Your Taxable Estate:	$1,000,000	$2,500,000	$5,000,000	$10,000,000
Year:				
1998	143,750	823,750	2,188,750	4,938,750
2000	125,250	805,250	2,170,250	4,920,250
2006	0	680,000	2,045,000	4,795,000

Tax Planning for Charitable Gifts – A Special Rule

A Special Rule

Congress has provided a special rule in the tax code having to do with charitable gifts of appreciated property. In many situations, taking advantage of this rule will be of *no use* to a donor and will not save any money. But in *some* situations *this might be the smart choice to make.*

Remember that under the *general* rule, a taxpayer who makes a charitable contribution of property can deduct the value of that gift up to 30% of income. Under the *special* rule, a taxpayer who makes a charitable gift of appreciated property *can choose to reduce the amount of the deduction to the cost or basis of the property*, and one important new rule will follow: the value of the gift (as reduced to basis) will be deductible *up to 50% of the taxpayer's income*, compared to the 30% ceiling without the election.

The decision to use the new rule is made by making an "election" to reduce the value of the gift to basis, and to increase the deduction to 50% of income. The "election" is made on a statement filed with your tax return. Your advisor can help you with the details.

When to Consider the Special Rule: Little or No Appreciation

In certain situations, it seems clear that making the election may be the right thing to do. One such situation occurs when a gift of property or of an easement is made either shortly after acquiring the property, either by purchase or inheritance (when there has been a "stepped-up basis," as discussed in Chapter 7), or when there has not been any significant increase in the value of the property. But don't assume anything!! Run the numbers!!

Example 1

In January, 1996, John and Mary acquire Riverview for $390,000. In February, 1998, when Riverview is valued at $420,000, John and Mary donate an easement that lowers the value of Riverview to $280,000. The value of the easement is $140,000, and its basis is $130,000 (one-third of Riverview's basis of $390,000).

John and Mary have annual income of $120,000 and other deductions of $35,000 ($10,000 in state income tax and $25,000 in mortgage interest). The $140,000 easement deduction is used up in four years.

Without the Donation

	Years 1-4
Income	$120,000
Deductions	$35,000
Tax Due	$16,960

With the Donation and Without the Election

	Years 1-3	Year 4
Income	$120,000	$120,000
Deductions	$71,000	$67,000
Tax Due	$6,880	$8,000

With the Donation and With the Election

	Years 1-2	Year 3	Year 4
Income	$120,000	$120,000	$120,000
Deductions	$95,000	$45,000	$35,000
Tax Due	$2,955	$14,160	$16,960

Income Tax Savings, *without* Election:	$39,200
Income Tax Savings, *with* Election:	$30,810

Note that with the election the tax savings are significantly higher in the first two years. Once again, *this example illustrates the importance of running the numbers and the value of good planning.*

Example 2

A similar opportunity to accelerate the income tax savings exists in the case of the "conservation buyer," the buyer who is willing to pay a premium for a valuable piece of land but who does not want to develop that land. The buyer may be someone who has had an enormously successful financial year, from a rock star to a lottery winner, or any other wealthy individual who can afford to pay top dollar.

Let's assume Mr. Entrepreneur, whose annual income is normally in the $200,000 to $400,000 a year range, has just sold a block of stock in the company he began ten years ago, and his taxable income this year jumps to $3,500,000. Mr. and Mrs. Entrepreneur buy Riverview, John and Mary's 200-acre estate, for $2,500,000. Mr. and Mrs. Entrepreneur then donate a conservation easement on Riverview, prohibiting any further development, and the value of Riverview is reduced to $1,000,000.

Since there has been no increase in the value of Riverview since Mr. and Mrs. Entrepreneur acquired it, *all* $1,500,000 of the deduction is basis. Mr. and Mrs. Entrepreneur make the election, and these are the results for the year of the donation (assume no other deductions).

Without the Donation

	Year 1
Income	$3,500,000
Tax Due	$695,880

With the Donation and the Election

	Year 1
Income	$3,500,000
Deduction	$1,353,636
Tax Due	$416,153
Income Tax Savings:	$279,727

It does not matter whether Mr. and Mrs. Entrepreneur are motivated by a strong conservation ethic or by tax savings or both. The result is the same in either case. A wealthy buyer with a significant amount of taxable income can help "finance" the acquisition of desirable property in this manner; a "conservation buyer" can acquire a sensitive and important piece of land that comes on the market, land that perhaps is being sold by an estate (before the property owner had a chance to read this book), and can help "finance" the protection of that land with this same technique.

When Else to Consider the Election

There are a lot of variables involved in tax planning. It is often difficult to generalize about when to make the election and sometimes it is unwise to generalize. But it often makes sense *simply to run the numbers to determine whether some additional income tax savings would be available with the election.* One specific situation in which the election should be considered is when the donors (or donor) are quite elderly or in such poor health that the potential benefits of a five-year carryforward of the income tax deduction may never be realized.

The following example illustrates the case of an elderly donor and also illustrates some of the variables, and some of the choices, involved in tax planning.

Example 3

Mary Landowner is 85 and a widow. She has a large annual income from investments and $25,000 in deductions ($15,000 in state income tax, $5,000 in property tax, and $5,000 in mortgage interest). Let's assume in this case that Riverview has a basis of $550,000 and is currently valued at $1,000,000. Let's also assume that an easement prohibiting any further development on Riverview would be valued at $600,000 and would therefore have a basis of $330,000 (60% of Riverview's basis of $550,000).

Without the Donation

	Years 1-6
Income	$300,000
Deductions	$19,636
Tax Due	$90,037

With the Donation and Without the Election

	Years 1-6
Income	$300,000
Deductions	$109,636
Tax Due	$57,302

With the Donation and With the Election

	Years 1-2	Year 3
Income	$300,000	$300,000
Deductions	$169,636	$49,636
Tax Due	$35,702	$78,902

Income Tax Savings, *without* Election:	$196,410
Income Tax Savings, *with* Election:	$119,805
Income Tax Savings, Years 1-2, *without* Election:	$65,470
Income Tax Savings, Years 1-2, *with* Election:	$108,670

The numbers speak for themselves. In this situation, of course, the decision whether or not to make the election is a particularly personal one for each donor.

Comments and Observations

Once again, as with most of the other tax consequences of charitable conservation giving, generalizations can only go so far. Further, what makes sense with the same income and deductions each year may not make sense if a landowner expects significant financial changes from one year to the next. Clearly, there is no substitute for good counsel and for "running the numbers." The election may be useful and appropriate only in certain circumstances, but it is up to each donor to determine whether his or her situation is one of them.

An Important Estate Tax Incentive for Landowners

Observations to Start

In 1997, for the first time in more than a decade, Congress added to the law significant new tax incentives for voluntary land protection by private landowners. Let's start with a few important observations.

1. Every single conservation easement must now take into account the provisions of the new law as part of the planning process.

2. Every single family lands situation must now take into account the provisions of the new law as part of the planning process.

3. Many conservation easements that have already been recorded should now be reviewed because of the provisions of the new law.

4. The new law will make planning immediately after the death of many landowners complex, difficult, expensive, possibly highly beneficial, and *absolutely necessary.*

5. With proper comprehensive planning, owners of important land can protect that land and save many more estate tax dollars than was possible under the old law.

Background

In mid-1997, President Clinton signed into law the Taxpayer Relief Act of 1997. Most of the commentary on that legislation focused on the cut in the capital gains rate to 20%, education and retirement-saving incentives, and lower estate tax rates for individuals and some family-owned businesses.

For landowners, however, there is more news and good news. The new legislation also included a modified version of The American Farm and Ranch Protection Act, an important new tax incentive for landowners.

The original version of The American Farm and Ranch Protection Act was first introduced in Congress in 1990 by Senator John Chafee and Congressman Richard Schulze. The proposal originated with the Piedmont Environmental Council (PEC), based in northern Virginia. Some PEC supporters and representatives became convinced of the need for additional tax code incentives for land protection and came up with the following simple, direct proposal for relief: land subject to a conservation easement under Section 170(h) of the tax code should be totally exempt from estate tax. That was essentially the provision introduced by Senator Chafee and Congressman Schulze in 1990. Over the next several years, as the federal legislative process moved forward, the proposal became more complex and less comprehensive. However, it remains an important new incentive for private, voluntary land conservation that landowners, their advisors, and land trusts must become familiar with.

How the New Law Works

The American Farm and Ranch Protection Act added to the tax code a new Section 2031(c), "Estate Tax With Respect to Land Subject to a Qualified Conservation Easement."

Before we review the specific rules of Section 2031(c), let us clarify what this all means and what it doesn't mean.

It does mean that all of the existing conservation easement rules of Section 170(h), the current conservation easement section, are still intact and that Section 170(h) works exactly the same way it did before the 1997 tax code changes. If you donate an easement on land you own, and if the easement meets the requirements of Section 170(h), you are entitled to an income tax deduction for the value of the conservation easement. In addition, the value of the land is reduced for estate tax purposes. It makes no difference under the new statute whether you donated the easement *during your lifetime*, or, as discussed in Chapter 5, in your will.

After you have met the requirements of Section 170(h), then you can look at the additional benefits potentially available under Section 2031(c). However, at this point two things can happen. First, and more on this below, it is entirely possible that even though your easement qualified under Section 170(h) your situation may not be eligible for the additional benefits of Section 2031(c). Second, your situation may be eligible for the benefits of Section 2031(c) but for tax or other reasons the executor of your estate may decide not to elect Section 2031(c).

Put another way, an easement *must qualify* under Section 170(h) to be eligible for the benefits of Section 2031(c), but if the easement *doesn't* qualify under Section 2031(c) that has no impact whatsoever on qualification for all of the benefits of Section 170(h).

In a nutshell, this is what new Section 2031(c) says: if you have land subject to a conservation easement that meets the requirements of Section 170(h), and if you own that land when you die, and if you meet the requirements of Section 2031(c), then you can exclude *an additional percentage of the value of that land* from your estate in addition to the reduction in value already attributable to the easement. Here are the important parts of new Section 2031(c).

I.   The new law will allow an executor to elect to exclude from a decedent's estate for federal estate tax purposes up to 40% of the value of land (not structures) subject to a conservation easement if:

- the land is within a 25-mile radius of a Metropolitan Statistical Area, as defined by the Office of Management and Budget (typically an area with a population over 50,000), or a national park or wilderness area, or within 10 miles of an Urban National Forest;

- the easement was donated, is perpetual, and otherwise meets the requirements of Section 170(h). Easements qualifying solely because they protect historic assets are not eligible for Section 2031(c) benefits;

- the land was owned by the decedent or a member of the decedent's family for at least three years immediately prior to the decedent's death;

- the easement was donated by the decedent or a member of the decedent's family; and

- the easement prohibits all but minimal commercial recreational use of the land (see more on this point below).

If you are not certain whether your land falls within the geographic limitations of Section 2031(c) discussed above, contact the Land Trust Alliance in Washington, D.C. (see Chapter 8), for assistance on this point.

II. The maximum amount that may be excluded from an estate under the new provisions is $100,000 in 1998, increasing by $100,000 each year up to the maximum exclusion of $500,000 in 2002 and thereafter. The exclusion applies regardless of when the easement was donated.

Here is the simplest possible example of how the new exclusion will work.

John owns land worth $2,000,000. In 1998, he donates a qualifying conservation easement that reduces the value of his land to $1,000,000. He dies in 2003. The land is valued in his estate at $1,000,000. His executor elects to take the Section 2031(c) exclusion; 40% of the $1,000,000 land value is excluded from John's estate; $600,000 of land value is subject to estate tax.

Note that if the planning is done correctly, the estates of *both spouses* can be eligible for the new Section 2031(c) exclusion.

III. "Development rights" retained in the easement *will* be subject to estate tax. Neither the statute nor the congressional committee reports answer all the questions about exactly what is a development right. The statute defines "development right" as a right that is retained for any commercial purpose which is "not subordinate to and directly supportive of the use of such land" for farming, ranching, etc., purposes. Reserved rights to continue agricultural, farming, ranching, and forestry activities *are permissible* and are clearly not development rights. The right to subdivide and convey additional house lots (of whatever size) clearly *is a development right* and clearly will be subject to estate tax (although see more on this point below). The right to own and maintain an existing residence is not a development right.

However, development rights retained in the easement *will not be subject to estate tax* (which is due nine months after the decedent's death) if within nine months of the decedent's death the heirs of the property agree to give up permanently some or all of those development rights. Those rights do not actually have to be given up within nine months; the heirs have nine months *to agree to eliminate them* and then have up to two years after the decedent's death to give up those rights.

Some landowners and/or donee organizations prefer leaving potential future house lot sites outside of the tract of land to be covered by a conservation easement. The ability to retain *or extinguish* those rights may make it prudent to include them under the easement. This can provide a very important "second look," for estate planning purposes, after the landowner's death. In fact, if the extinguishment of the development rights takes the form of a conservation easement that meets the requirements of Section 170(h), the conservation easement section, the heirs may be entitled to an income tax deduction.

"Development rights" are not the same as commercial recreational activities. A golf course is clearly a commercial recreational activity, and Congress did not want a landowner to be able to reserve this sort of activity under an easement and still benefit from the Section 2031(c) exclusion. If an easement *does not prohibit* all but what the law calls "de minimis" commercial recreational activities the estate will not be eligible for the Section 2031(c) exclusion.

IV. If there is a mortgage on the property, an amount of land value equal to the amount of the indebtedness will not be eligible for the exclusion. In other words, if land subject to an easement is worth $1,000,000, but there is a $300,000 mortgage on the property, only $700,000 of the land value will be eligible for the exclusion. Of course, the mortgage will usually be deductible as a debt of the estate.

V. To the extent the estate takes the exclusion, land will retain the same basis as it had in the hands of the landowner/decedent, rather than being entitled to a stepped-up basis, for calculating any gain on a subsequent sale. These terms need a brief explanation.

The concept of "basis" is a tax law concept. In many (but not all) situations, for tax purposes "basis" and "cost" mean the same thing. This is a very simple illustration, but if you buy stock for $1,000 and sell it for $2,000, you will pay tax on the $1,000 gain, which is the difference between what you sold it for and your basis of $1,000.

If you hold that stock until you die, the estate tax will be based on the $2,000 value of that stock. However, when your children inherit the stock it will have a basis in their hands of $2,000. The tax law refers to this as a "stepped-up basis," and this was covered briefly in Chapter 7. If the children sell it for $2,000, there will be no tax on the gain (but remember that there was an estate tax on the $2,000 value). Once again, to the extent an estate takes advantage of the exclusion, a portion of the basis of the land would not be "stepped up" but would remain the same as it was in the hands of the decedent; that is, it would be "carried over."

VI. The exclusion is available when land is owned by family corporations, partnerships, or trusts as long as the decedent owned at least a 30% interest in the corporation, partnership, or trust at the time of death.

VII. The amount of the exclusion will be reduced below 40% by two percentage points for each one percentage point by which the easement fails to reduce the value of the land by 30%. This complicated rule is intended to discourage "marginal" easements that don't reduce the value of land very much, although the percentage reduction in value often has little or nothing to do with the importance of the conservation values to be protected by the easement.

Here is how this rule works. If land is worth $1,000,000 without an easement and, say, $650,000 subject to an easement, the full 40% exclusion under the statute will apply because the easement reduced the value of the land by more than 30%. On the other hand, if the easement reduced the value of the land from $1,000,000 to $800,000, because this 20% reduction in value is ten percentage points less than 30%, the exclusion is reduced from 40% to 20% (two percentage points for each point the easement fails to reduce the land value by 30%).

Put another way, if an easement reduces land value from $1,000,000 to $650,000, using the exclusion the total value subject to estate tax will be $390,000 ($650,000 minus 40% of $650,000). If the easement reduces land value from $1,000,000 to $800,000, using the exclusion the total value subject to estate tax will be $640,000 ($800,000 minus 20% of $800,000). These examples assume the maximum individual exclusion amount of $500,000 is fully phased in.

One obviously critical issue that has come up about the way this particular rule works is the question of whether the 30% reduction in value is to be calculated on the date the easement was donated (assuming the donation was made during the landowner's lifetime) or on the date of the decedent's death. Although making the determination on the date of the donation would ensure certainty, it now appears that the calculation will need to be made *as of the date of the landowner's death.* Although there is very little data on this, in the vast majority of cases the evidence seems to indicate that once an easement is donated the percentage reduction in value attributable to the easement is not likely to decrease. In fact, the value of the easement seems likely to increase as development pressure and real estate values in the area increase.

There may be additional legislative efforts to change this rule to a date-of-donation determination, but for now a date-of-death calculation seems likely.

"Post-Mortem" Easement Donation (Easement Donation After the Death of the Landowner)

Prior to the new law, if a landowner died without having either donated an easement during lifetime or including an easement donation in his or her will, the estate tax was based on the full, unrestricted, fair market value of the land. The new law includes a very important provision that will allow executors and trustees to elect to donate a qualified conservation easement *after the death of the land-owner.* This is a so-called "post-mortem" or "after-death" easement donation.

The legal rules on when and under what circumstances an executor or heirs can make such a donation can vary widely from state to state, and may require changes in some state laws under some circumstances. In some states, for example, title to real estate vests in the *heirs* as of the date of death, while in other states the executor of the estate may hold title. It is important to check with your advisors on this and any other state law issues concerning the post-mortem easement donation.

If state law issues can be satisfactorily addressed, here is the simplest possible example of how the post-mortem donation will work.

John owns land worth $2,000,000. He did not donate an easement during his lifetime and he did not include an easement in his will. He dies in 2003 and leaves the land to his children. The land is valued in his estate at $2,000,000. His executor and his children agree to donate a conservation easement; the easement reduces the value of his land to $1,000,000 and that $1,000,000 of value is subject to estate tax. *In addition*, his executor elects to take the Section 2031(c) exclusion; an additional 40% of the $1,000,000 land value is excluded from John's estate, with the result that $600,000 of land value is subject to estate tax. (Under these circumstances, even though the easement met the requirements of Section 170(h), the easement rules, apparently neither the estate nor the children will be able to take an *income tax deduction* for donating the easement.)

Commercial Recreational Activities

Here is another important post-mortem planning opportunity. Assume Mary dies owning land restricted by an easement that met the requirements of Section 170(h) but that the easement does not prohibit commercial recreational activity and therefore the estate is ineligible for the Section 2031(c) exclusion. Since the executor can in fact make a post-mortem *easement donation* in order to qualify for Section 2031(c) benefits, it also appears that the executor can make a post-mortem *easement amendment* in order to eliminate any prohibited commercial recreational activity so as to be eligible for Section 2031(c).

Note of Caution

The post-mortem easement donation and the post-mortem easement amendment are important. However, while these planning opportunities are useful additions to the planner's toolbox, a landowner or a family should not take the position that comprehensive planning during lifetime should be put off because of the availability of post-mortem planning opportunities. For one thing, the law is *absolutely clear* on the income tax and estate tax savings that are available when an easement is donated during lifetime. All the issues are *not clear* in the case of a post-mortem donation. In addition, using these post-mortem tools successfully means addressing a complex array of state law and other related questions and reaching agreement among all necessary parties within a relatively short period after the death of the decedent. It is certainly better to see to it that the proper planning is done during the lifetime of the landowner.

Another Important Change To The Tax Rules

The 1997 Tax Act also included estate tax relief for many family-owned small businesses, and farming, ranching, and forestry activities that are run as family businesses may be able to qualify for relief under these provisions. The combined effect of the new estate tax rules and the family business relief provision is that *with proper planning* up to $1,300,000 in value can be passed on with no estate tax from an individual's estate when a qualifying business is involved and when the fairly complex and technical provisions of this new family business benefit are met. The new Section 2031(c) provisions can be *added on top of this*;

in other words, *with proper planning*, with a qualifying land-based business, and once all of the new relief provisions are fully phased in, it appears that up to $1,800,000 in value can be excluded from an individual's estate, that is, $1,300,000 from using the general estate tax provisions and the family business provisions and $500,000 from new Section 2031(c).

Although it certainly appears that both spouses can take advantage of the Section 2031(c) exclusion (potentially doubling the estate tax benefit), it is not clear at this point the extent to which *both* spouses can take advantage of *all* of these benefits. However, *at an absolute minimum* and *with proper planning*, owners of important land can save many more estate tax dollars than was possible under the old law. The key words in the previous sentences are "*with proper planning.*" Once again, planning during lifetime to qualify for these benefits is critical.

Planning Observations To Conclude

1. Land that falls outside the geographic limitations of new Section 2031(c) simply will not be eligible for the benefits of that section. However, continued urban sprawl will inevitably result in the addition of new Metropolitan Statistical Areas to the map, and that will mean greater coverage under Section 2031(c).

2. Every single conservation easement must now take into account the provisions of Section 2031(c) as part of the planning process. Retained development rights can be extinguished after the death of the landowner, but more than "de minimis" retained commercial recreational rights *can disqualify the easement* from Section 2031(c) eligibility.

3. Every single family lands planning situation must now take into account the provisions of Section 2031(c) as part of the planning process. Do the current owners want to gift the property to children over a period of years as part of the estate planning and succession planning process? Does the family want to remain eligible for the Section 2031(c) benefits? There is no "right" answer to these questions, but now we have an important additional planning tool in the landowner's toolbox.

4. Every recorded easement should be reviewed with Section 2031(c) eligibility in mind (to look for a prohibition on commercial recreational activities, for example) if the land is still owned by the same family that donated the easement.

5. One of the "costs" of the new Section 2031(c) benefit is that planning after death becomes much more complicated. Experienced appraisers will need to be available to give the family accurate valuation numbers (land value before and after the easement for purposes of the 30% test, the post-mortem election, and the value of retained development rights) in sufficient time for the family to make an informed judgment about what to do. In connection with the new post-mortem easement provision, a conservation easement that satisfies state law rules and has the agreement of all necessary parties must be successfully completed after the decedent's death.

New Section 2031(c) is a very important incentive for land conservation. It will take some time to sort out all of the planning issues, and to answer some of the planning questions that have already come up, but landowners and their advisors and land trusts must begin to work with the new law. Saving important land and saving tax dollars is a tough combination to beat!

Note: this Appendix is adapted from an article that I co-authored for "Exchange," a quarterly publication of the Land Trust Alliance, along with L. Timothy Lindstrom, Staff Attorney for the Piedmont Environmental Council.

ORDER FORM
Please cut along line at left and enclose with your check

You can order *Preserving Family Lands: Book I* or
Preserving Family Lands: Book II as follows:

Single Copy Orders:
    $14.95 per copy (includes postage and handling)

Bulk Orders:
    30-99 of the <u>same book</u>   @$6.00, plus shipping and handling
    100 or more of the <u>same book</u>   @$5.00, plus shipping and handling

Shipping and Handling for bulk orders:
    30-50 copies $35.00
    51-99 copies $45.00
    100-150 copies $55.00
    151-200 copies $65.00

    Please call 617-357-1644 for shipping charges for quantities over 200.

☐ I would like to order _____ copies of *Preserving Family Lands: Book I*
    at $ _____ per copy.
☐ I would like to order _____ copies of *Preserving Family Lands: Book II*
    at $ _____ per copy.

Total dollar amount for copies ordered   _____
Shipping and handling charges (bulk orders only)   _____
5% MA Sales Tax (for orders shipped to Massachusetts addresses) _____
                                            TOTAL: _____

Please send to the following address:

Name: _____

Affiliation or Business (if applicable): _____

Street: _____

City, State, Zip Code: _____

Please Note: We ship by UPS. If you are ordering more than ten (10) copies, please
use a street address since <u>UPS will NOT deliver to a Post Office Box</u>.

A CHECK FOR THE FULL AMOUNT MUST ACCOMPANY YOUR ORDER.
Please make check out to "Preserving Family Lands" and mail to:

Preserving Family Lands
PO Box 2242
Boston, MA 02107

Prices may be subject to change